The Family Formula Book

by Cicely Nichols

Publishers • GROSSET & DUNLAP • New York
A FILMWAYS COMPANY

Copyright © 1978 by Grosset & Dunlap, Inc.
All rights reserved
Published simultaneously in Canada
ISBN 0-448-14360-7 (hardcover edition)
ISBN 0-448-14361-5 (paperback edition)
Library of Congress catalog card number: 77-78923
First printing 1978
Printed in the United States of America

Introduction

Last year, my friend Judy read a book that gave formulas, or recipes, for making your own cosmetics. Judy has fine, wispy, fly-away hair, and there was a formula for a conditioner that would add body to hair; so Judy stirred it up and tried it.

Quite a mess: Her hair was stiff and sticky; it felt awful and it looked worse. Judy decided, naturally, that the thing to do was wash it—and then she was more than dismayed to find that the conditioner would not wash out. She tried two or three different shampoos, and nothing worked; she wore a scarf over her hair for days; finally, she called a dermatologist. At his office, she told him what she'd tried to do, and showed him the formula. "Gelatin," he said—there was powdered gelatine in the formula—"is all very well for eating, but never, never put it on your hair."

I told Georg Zappler and Diana Price—editors at Grosset & Dunlap—about Judy and her hair, and we have kept that awful story in mind through all the work on *The Family Formula Book*. We have checked and double-checked, and solicited the advice of scientists—because this book is meant to be useful. It is also meant to be safe, so you will see the word caution in this book quite a bit.

Safety was also our concern when we decided to include the list of "Common Drug Interactions." For instance, your doctor and/or your pharmacist should tell you—but very often he or she does not—that when you are taking the antibiotic tetracycline, you should not drink milk. Also, tetracycline often causes an upset stomach in some patients—which prompts the patient to take one of the non-prescription digestive aids such as Tums or Maalox; but Tums or Maalox or certain other antacids tend to make the tetracycline ineffective.

Some research has been done that tends to show that food additives—chemicals that many food processors add to change color or increase shelf-life, among other things—are a major cause of what's called "hyperactivity" in children. A great many scientists have questioned the wisdom of taking into our bodies the great array of added chemicals, bleaches, preservatives, and so on, that are not naturally present in wholesome food and are put in for economic, not nutritional, reasons. Too often, scientists find out that some substance we haven't paid attention to is harmful—after we've been eating it or breathing it for years. The label doesn't always tell you what has been added and the labels on certain breads and certain cheeses, although they look informative, can actually be disguising the presence of additives. Whether you decide to avoid additives or not, we tell you in Part II how to tell when you're being lied to.

We also tell you how to save money buying eggs; how to save money—and avoid additives—making your own pancake mix, biscuit mix, salad dressing mix, and instant breakfasts. There's a method for defrosting the freezer that will make that unpleasant chore go much faster. There's a method for oven cleaning that's both painless and inexpensive, and almost effortless—and you don't need to buy spray cans. There's a chicken receipe that tastes like Colonel Sanders' chicken—and two easy recipes that will save you from buying packages of Shake 'n' Bake.®

The car, the lawn, the garden, insects, and your gas and electric bills come in for their share of attention, too—so does your personal care—your hair, your skin, and the calories you eat.

A few of the formulas here are included just for fun; most of those came from a yellowed, crumbling volume titled *The Handy Home Book*. It was published in Canada, but it doesn't say when; there is a clue, though: It has a list in it called "Faiths of U.S. Presidents," and the most recent one included is President Theodore Roosevelt (Dutch Reformed). "Making a Bearskin Rug" is from that source, and I put it in just for fun, but one of the editors had just recently cured a fox skin, and was quite seriously interested in the bear-skin method.

Whether a formula was included for fun or for serious reasons, it has been carefully checked for effectiveness and safety. The two consultants who worked most closely on *The Family Formula Book* were Neil Nichols, who is both my brother and an electrical engineer, Registered Professional Engineer, Electrical, State of California; and Jerome Sandler, who brought to the book a B.S. in pharmacy, B.S. in electrical engineering, M.S. in electronic engineering, and Ph.D. in oceanography. Their help was both necessary and invaluable, and is very much appreciated.

Our aim is that *The Family Formula Book* will help your family's budget and help your family's health. We hope that you will find following these formulas a pleasure, too.

I should note that the dermatologist was eventually able to remove the gelatin from Judy's hair. Since then, Judy has been using skim milk on her hair (in the way described on page 4) successfully.

Editor's Note

Some of the formulas in this book call for the use of substances which can be caustic, toxic, or flammable. We have made every effort to see that each substance that is dangerous or potentially dangerous has been noted as such, and have included cautions with all formulas that require special care in preparation. Consultation with your pharmacist is recommended if you are in any doubt.

All preparations should be labeled carefully; and all should be kept out of reach of children or pets.

Caution: *When you are mixing a formula that calls for an undiluted substance, remember that if it is a caustic material, it will be much more so in the concentrated form. A splash or a spill can do a great deal of damage with such substances—the human body is vulnerable. When you see a* ▲ *next to a formula, that means there is a special cautionary note.*

MEASUREMENTS

In many of these formulas, the dry ingredients are called for by volume, by the teaspoon or the cup. Dry things that are called for by the ounce or the pound—such as the potassium hydroxide in the liquid shampoo on page 3—must be weighed on a scale. A postage scale would do. Caustic or acid products should be weighed twice or three times to be sure of accuracy, because a postage scale's sensitivity can be questionable.

Liquids in the formulas should be measured by volume, not by weight. You can use the list below to convert the measurements to whatever instruments are most convenient for you. For instance, when a formula calls for 6 ounces of a liquid, you can see by checking below that it could be 36 teaspoons, or (preferably—for accuracy) ¾ cup.

Volume Measuring

The following will be most accurate if you use standard measuring cups and measuring spoons. Some common metric measurements are included, since we are in the process of changing to the metric system.

1 teaspoon	⅙ ounce
1 teaspoon	5 milliliters
1 teaspoon	100 drops
1 tablespoon	½ ounce
1 tablespoon	15 milliliters
1 tablespoon	3 teaspoons
1 cup	8 ounces
1 cup	240 milliliters
1 cup	48 teaspoons
1 cup	16 tablespoons
1 pint	480 milliliters
1 pint	96 teaspoons
1 pint	32 tablespoons
1 pint	2 cups
1 medicine dropper	about 20 drops
1 medicine dropper	about 1 milliliter
1 ounce	30 milliliters
1 ounce	2 tablespoons
1 ounce	6 teaspoons
1 quart	2 pints
1 quart	4 cups
1 gallon	4 quarts

Contents

PART I Caring for Yourself and Your Family
    PERSONAL CARE *3*
    BABY CARE *12*
    MEDICINES, DRUGS, AND SIMPLE REMEDIES *13*

PART II The Foods You Eat
    BREAD, CAKES, AND COOKIES *25*
    CEREALS *27*
    CHEESE *28*
    COFFEE STRETCHERS AND COFFEE SUBSTITUTES *33*
    EGGS *34*
    FLOURS *34*
    FRUITS AND FRUIT DRINKS *35*
    WINE MAKING *37*
    HERBS AND SEASONINGS *38*
    JELLIES, GELATINS, AND BUTTERS *38*
    MEAT, POULTRY, AND FISH *40*
    MILK AND MILK PRODUCTS *48*
    PANCAKES *52*
    SALAD DRESSINGS *53*
    VEGETABLES, PASTA, AND RICE *56*

viii / Contents

PART III In the House

    DRAINS *65*
    FIREPLACES *65*
    GLASS *66*
    HOUSEPLANTS *67*
    MARBLE *69*
    PETS *70*
    FIREARMS *71*
    FABRIC CARE *72*
    FURS *75*
    LEATHER *76*
    SOAP *78*
    WALLPAPER *78*
    WHITEWASH *79*
    WOOD *79*
    METAL *82*
    LIGHTER FLUID *84*
    OVENS *84*
    PORCELAIN *85*
    REFRIGERATORS AND FREEZERS *85*
    PIANOS *85*
    BOOKS *86*
    CANDLES *87*
    ANIMAL HORNS *87*

PART IV Controlling Household Pests 89

PART V In the Garden

    PLANTS THAT HELP AND NEED HELP *107*
    GENERAL CARE *115*
    LAWNS *117*
    GUIDE FOR SELECTING FUNGICIDES *121*

BIRDS *125*
DOG AND CAT REPELLENTS *127*
AUTOMOBILE CARE *127*

PART VI Energy, Safety, and Miscellaneous Formulas

ENERGY *131*
FIRE RETARDATION *137*
HUMIDITY INDICATOR *141*
SETTING CLOCKS *141*
SWIMMING POOL DISINFECTION *141*
DUSTPROOFING EARTH FOR TRACKS AND TENNIS COURTS *141*

PART VII Arts and Crafts

CORNSTARCH "CERAMICS" *145*
NONHARDENING MODELING CLAY *145*
PLAY-DOUGH FOR CHILDREN *145*
FLOWER CARE *145*
DECORATING GLASS *146*
PAINT FOR CRAFTWORK OR FINGER PAINTING *147*
PAPIER-MACHE *147*
PLASTER CASTS *147*
ENGRAVING STEEL *148*
CLEANING OLD COINS *149*
CANDLES *149*
SEASHELLS *149*

INDEX 151

Part I.

Caring for Yourself and Your Family

PERSONAL CARE
Hair Care

Dry Shampoo

When you want clean hair, but don't want to wet your hair (because there's not enough time, or because you have a cold), brush a handful of cornmeal through your hair. This will remove dirt and oil and leave your hair feeling freshly washed.

▲Conditioner for Dry Hair

After shampooing and rinsing, dry hair with a towel. Rub mayonnaise into the hair along with 1 tablespoon collagenous hydrolyzed protein and leave these on 30 to 60 minutes. Shampoo again (lightly), and finally rinse with vinegar-water—2 tablespoons apple-cider vinegar to each quart of water.

▲**Caution:** *Be sure the mayonnaise is only egg, oil, and vinegar or lemon juice. See page 53 for information on hidden additives that could be damaging to hair and page 54 for pure-mayonnaise recipes.*

Conditioner for Dry Scalp and Brittle Hair

After the second soaping, using an acid-balanced protein shampoo, dry hair with a towel and apply the following mixture:

½ ounce apple-cider vinegar
½ ounce glycerin
½ ounce corn oil or wheat-germ oil

3 ounces collagenous hydrolyzed protein

Leave the mixture on at least 20 minutes, then rinse.

Wave Set or Body-builder for Hair

1 cup flaxseed   3 cups water

Boil the flaxseed—ground or whole—in the water, then cool until it forms a jelly. Dilute with more water if desired. Use after shampooing—after the first rinse and before the last rinse.

or

Rinse the hair normally after shampooing, then use skim milk as a final rinse and allow hair to dry.

or

Make a paste with nonfat dry milk and water, apply it to the hair, and leave on 20 minutes.

or

Rub in wheat-germ oil, then rinse it out with vinegar-water—2 tablespoons apple-cider vinegar to each quart water.

Rinse after Peroxiding Hair

One beauty expert recommends dissolving a small amount of brewer's yeast in the final rinse water used after a peroxide treatment, in order to prevent the fading of hair color.

Restoring Hair Damaged by a Permanent

After shampooing and rinsing, rub blackstrap molasses into the hair and leave it on 1 hour, then rinse with vinegar-water—2 tablespoons apple-cider vinegar to each quart of water.

Increasing Red Highlights in Dark Hair

1 cup chopped parsley   2 cups water

Boil the parsley in the water for a few minutes, cool, strain, and use the liquid as a final rinse.

Gradual Color for Gray Hair

1 tablespoon dried sage leaves
4 tablespoons leftover tea leaves

Add water to make 2 cups, simmer 30 minutes, cool, strain, and use as final rinse.

Hands and Nails

Preventive Hand Care

Rub a cake of soap all over the hands and wrists (with special attention to fingernails—get soap under them) before starting work with greasy and dirty materials—it will eliminate or at least reduce staining on your hands.

Heavy-Duty Hand Soap

1¼ ounces borax
1 ounce washing soda
½ ounce glycerin
5 ounces powdered soap
7 ounces powdered pumice
13 ounces water

Dissolve the borax, washing soda, and glycerin in 3 ounces of the water, then dissolve the powdered soap in the rest of the water. Stir the solutions together, then stir in the pumice.

Hand Lotion

¼ ounce gum tragacanth
2 ounces glycerin
1 ounce bay rum
½ ounce perfume

Soak the gum tragacanth overnight in 1 cup warm water; in the morning, beat with a fork or eggbeater, getting air into it. Add the glycerin, bay rum, and your favorite perfume; beat again.

Glycerin Hand Lotion

8 ounces glycerin   8 ounces rosewater

Mix together. Store in a tightly capped bottle. (This is the classic hand-lotion formula.)

Fingernail Conditioner and Whitener

Soak the tips of your fingers in 1 part lemon juice, 1 part olive oil.

▲ Nail-Polish Remover

½ cup acetone   ¼ teaspoon vegetable oil

Stir until thoroughly blended and store in a tightly stopped bottle.

Lizzy's Fingernail Strengthener

Empty the tea from a tea bag, and cut a piece of the gauze to fit the end of the fingernail; wet the gauze with clear nail polish until it is transparent. Fit the wetted gauze on the fingernail, let it dry in place, and paint it twice more with clear polish. The gauze won't show.

Mascara

Rita Moreno's Mascara

Let a wooden match burn, then crush it, and put what's left on your eyelashes.

Antiperspirant

Antiperspirant Solution

2 ounces aluminum chloride   8 ounces water

Combine and stir; store in a bottle with a tight cap to prevent waste through evaporation. This should be as effective for most users as the advertised commercial preparations.

▲ **Caution:** *Acetone is highly flammable.*

Skin Care

A Drink for Improving the Complexion

The chief cook for England's royal family wrote: "There is one secret which may provide a clue to those flawless complexions—barley water. It was always on the dining table. In fact they drank so much that I felt there must be something in it and tried it myself. A day or two on barley water is wonderfully purifying ... does wonders for the skin."

½ cup pearl barley
2½ quarts boiling water
Rinds and juice of 2 lemons
Brown sugar or honey to taste
Rinds and juice of 6 oranges
(make sure these have no coloring or preservatives added)

Put the boiling water and barley in a large pot and simmer 1 hour at low heat, with the lid on. Then strain the barley water into a bowl; add the sugar or honey and the lemon and orange rinds. Let the mixture cool—then discard the rinds and add the fruit juice. Keep in refrigerator.

Lanolin Lotion for the Skin

½ ounce white powdered soap
5 ounces pure lanolin
¼ ounce borax
44 ounces water
Perfume as desired

Dissolve the borax and soap in the water, heated to about 110° F. Melt the lanolin separately; pour it into the water solution with vigorous stirring. Finally, add perfume. Shake before using.

Shaving

Brushless Shaving Cream

8 ounces heavy mineral oil
40 ounces water
8 ounces diglycol stearate

Heat oil and diglycol stearate to 150° F. in the top of a double boiler. Heat the water separately to the same temperature and stir slowly into the mixture. Let cool to lukewarm. Keep stirring until it is at room temperature. Store in bottles with tight caps.

After-Shave Lotion

½ ounce crystalline boric acid
15 ounces water

20 ounces ethyl rubbing alcohol compound (70 percent alcohol)

Stir the ingredients together; store in tightly capped bottles.

Dental Care

▲ Tooth Powder

1 part table salt or kosher salt   1 part baking soda

The chairman of the New York University Dental Center Department of Preventive Dentistry recommends kosher salt because the magnesium sulfate in ordinary table salt dehydrates the gums. The secretary of the American Dental Association Council on Dental Therapeutics disagrees with that precaution—there isn't enough magnesium sulfate in table salt to matter, he says.

This toothpowder is widely recommended by dentists for adult use—it should not be used by children, however, as children's teeth need fluorides to prevent decay.

▲ **Caution:** *Salt can be dangerous to children. Keep out of reach.*

▲ Foamy Tooth Powders

5 ounces precipitated chalk
1 ounce sodium bicarbonate

¾ ounce powdered soap
Flavor, as desired

Mix thoroughly and sift.

or

1 ounce powdered soap
19 ounces precipitated chalk
18 grains soluble saccharin

½ teaspoon oil of peppermint
¼ teaspoon oil of cinnamon
1 teaspoon methyl salicylate

Grind and mix *thoroughly* the saccharin, oils, and methyl salicylate with half the precipitated chalk. Mix the soap with the other half, then mix the two powders together and put through a fine sieve.

▲ **Caution:** *Methyl salicylate (oil of wintergreen) is poisonous unless used only as a very small part of a mixture of other substances, as here. Keep out of reach of children.*

Denture Cleaners

Brush the denture, then let it stand for 15 minutes or overnight in

4 teaspoons clear household ammonia	½ cup water
	or
¼ teaspoon trisodium phosphate	½ cup warm water
	or
½ teaspoon 5 percent sodium hypochlorite solution (Clorox, Rose-X, Purex, etc.)	½ cup water

Rinse thoroughly.

Denture Adhesive

3 ounces powdered gum tragacanth   1 ounce powdered karaya gum
¼ teaspoon sassafras oil

Shake the gums together in a dry bottle until thoroughly mixed. Add the oil and shake again until the oil has blended with the powders. Sprinkle sparingly on the denture.

Temporary Cement for Crowns

zinc oxide powder   oil of cloves

Blend the oil of cloves and the zinc oxide to make a stiff paste and apply it to the inside of the crown. Be sure that leftover old cement is scraped out of the crown as much as possible, and off the tooth—and be sure the crown and tooth are both dry, for best adhesion.

Soothing Your Nerves

Secular Mental Relaxation or Meditation

1. Sit in a quiet place, in a position that's comfortable.
2. Relax your muscles—from your feet, calves, thighs, hip muscles, stomach muscles, arms, chest, shoulder muscles, neck, to your head—and allow them to stay deeply relaxed.

3. Breathe through your nose, and become aware of your breathing—say the word "one" silently to yourself as you breathe out each time.
4. Continue 10 to 20 minutes. Open your eyes to look at the clock if you wish, but don't set an alarm. When you've finished, don't get up right away but sit for a few minutes with your eyes still closed; continue sitting a few minutes longer with eyes open before getting up. Some claim that this "exercise" has lowered blood pressure in hypertensive patients.

HERBAL BATHS FOR SOOTHING NERVES AND RELIEVING INSOMNIA

2 ounces balm leaves, 1 quart boiling-hot water; steep 15 minutes, then add to bath water.

or

7 ounces European angelica roots, 2 quarts cold water; bring to a boil, steep 5 minutes, then add to bath water.

or

3 ounces mother of thyme, 2 cups boiling hot water; steep 10 minutes, then add to bath water.

or

3 pounds young twigs or young green cones from spruce tree, 4 gallons cold water; let stand 24 hours, then boil in the same water 2 hours; add to bath water.

Energy Expenditure by a 150-Pound Person in Various Activities

ACTIVITY	CALORIES PER HOUR
Rest and Light Activity	**Up to 200**
Resting in bed or sleeping	75
Sitting	100
Sitting and reading	100
Sitting and eating	110
Standing	125
Driving a car	140

Standing and dusting...................................... 160
Washing clothes (using machines)........................... 170

Moderate Activity................................... **200-350**
Bicycling (5½ mph).. 210
Walking (2½ mph).. 210
Dressing.. 210
Taking a shower... 210
Gardening... 220
Canoeing (2½ mph)... 230
Shining shoes... 240
Golf.. 250
Lawn mowing (power mower)................................. 250
Bowling... 270
Lawn mowing (hand mower).................................. 270
Fencing... 300
Rowboating (2½ mph)....................................... 300
Making beds... 300
Swimming (¼ mph).. 300
Walking (3¾ mph).. 300
Badminton... 350
Horseback riding (trotting)............................... 350
Square dancing.. 350
Volleyball.. 350
Roller skating.. 350

Vigorous Activity................................... **over 350**
Mopping floors.. 360
Table tennis.. 360
Ditch digging (hand shovel)............................... 400
Ice skating (10 mph)...................................... 400
Wood chopping or sawing................................... 400
Tennis.. 420
Walking downstairs.. 430
Water skiing.. 480
Hill climbing (100 ft. per hr.)........................... 490
Skiing (10 mph)... 600
Squash and handball....................................... 600
Cycling (13 mph).. 660
Scull rowing (race)....................................... 840
Running (10 mph).. 900
Walking upstairs.. 1,140

BABY CARE

First-Year Diet Costs in Addition to Milk

Using common commercial products:

Baby cereals (from 2 weeks on)	$ 3.00
Strained fruits (from 1 month on)	22.00
Strained meats and vegetables, added one at a time (from 3 or 4 months until 6 or 7 months)	36.00
Egg yolks in jars (from 6 months on)	36.00
"Junior" dinners, replacing strained foods (from 6 or 7 months on)	71.00
Teething biscuits and prepared finger foods (from 7 or 8 months on)	13.00
Cans of baby orange juice and other juices (from 6 months on)	36.00
	$217.00

Using fresh and additive-free nutritious foods:

Bananas (from 1 month on)	$ 5.00
Lean meats and fish, introduced one at a time (from 4 or 6 months on)	22.00
Fresh and dried fruits (from 6 or 7 months on)	12.00
Fresh and frozen vegetables (from 6 or 7 months on)	14.00
Egg yolks (from 7 months on)	7.00
Fresh-squeezed orange and other juices (from 7 months on)—and frozen concentrated juices are also nutritious, and less expensive than the canned juice	20.00
Cooked cereals and porridges made from natural, unsprayed grains and nutritional yeast (from 7 or 8 months on)	1.00
Home-baked teething biscuits, breads (from 8 months on)	4.00
	$85.00

MEDICINES, DRUGS, AND SIMPLE REMEDIES
How to Read Prescription Latin

On the prescription	Meaning
a.	ear
a.a.	equal parts of each
a.c.	before meals
ad	to, up to
add	add
ad lib.	as required for preparation
agit.	shake
alb.	white
aq.	water
b.	twice
b.i.d.	twice a day
c.	with
caps.	capsule
chart.	paper, a powder in paper
chart. cerat.	waxed paper
chartul.	small paper
collyr.	eyewash
d.	a day
d.	a dose
da	give
d.t.d	give such doses
dieb. alt.	every other day
disp.	dispense
div.	divide
dos.	a dose
et	and
ex aq.	without water
e.m.p.	as directed
flav.	yellow
ft.	make
gtt.	a drop, drops

On the prescription	Meaning
hor.	an hour
h.s.	at bedtime
m.	mix
mitt.	send
no.	in number
non	not
non rep.	do not repeat
O.	a pint
ocul.	the eye
o.d.	in right eye
o.l.	in left eye
o.s.	in left eye
o.u.	in each eye
p.c.	after meals
per	by means of
p.o.	by mouth
placebo	to please or satisfy
p.r.n.	as needed
pro tus.	for the cough
q.i.d.	four times a day
qh	every hour
q4h	every four hours
q.s.	a sufficient quantity
Rx	take
sig.	label, let it be labeled
s.	without
s.a.	according to the art
s.c., sub cut.	under the skin
s.o.s.	if needed
ss.	halt
stat.	immediately
s.v.r.	alcohol
t.i.d.	three times a day
ut dict.	as directed
v.	or
virid.	green

Storage of Medicines

Store medicines at moderate temperature, unless the pharmacist says to refrigerate them, but keep them out of the sunlight, and out of the reach of children. Keep medicines in the container the pharmacist put them in—different containers can affect medicines.

NITROGLYCERIN TABLETS

Nitroglycerin tablets—which are also sold under the trade names Nitro-Bid, Nitroglyn, Nitrong, Nitrospan, and Nitrostat—need special care in packaging and storage. A test by Ralph Shangraw at the University of Maryland School of Pharmacy showed that three-month-old nitroglycerin tablets in a package had lost 84 percent of their potency—the label, which was inside the container, had absorbed ten tablets' worth of nitroglycerin; the cotton packed into the container had absorbed ⅓ of the potency in only one week. Nitroglycerin tablets should not be left open to the air, nor should they be packed with cotton or with the prescription label on the inside. Nitroglycerin tablets should not be in the same container with other drugs, either; aspirin, for one, can absorb it.

Common Drug Interactions

The drugs in the left-hand column often interact with those in the corresponding column on the right. Note that only the most common drug interactions are listed here. Any time you are prescribed a new drug, it is wisest to inform your physician and your pharmacist of what other drugs you are taking. This applies not only to prescription drugs: it is important to mention over-the-counter drugs such as antacids, cough and cold preparations, and all others as well. Some, but by no means all, of the more potentially dangerous interactions are marked with an asterisk (*).

Antacids	Acidic drugs (e.g., nitrofurantoin, nalidixic acid, and some sulfonamides), tetracyclines,* penicillin G, barbiturates
Anabolic steroids	Oxyphenbutazone (Tandearil), sulfonylureas (Orinase, Diabinese), insulin, phenformin (DBI), coumarin anticoagulants*

Barbiturates	Tricyclic antidepressants (amitriptyline, desipramine, doxepin, imipramine, nortriptyline, protriptyline, Elovil, Sinequan, Tofranil), griseofulvin, coumarin anticoagulants, digitalis glycosides (e.g., Lanoxin), methylphenidate (Ritalin), sulfonylureas (Orinase, Diabinese), ethyl alcohol (alcoholic beverages),* narcotics,* phenothiazines (e.g., Compazine, Thorazine, Stelazine), benzodiazepines (e.g., Librium, Valium), antihistamines, meprobamate (Miltown, Equanil), other hypnotics (e.g., glutethimide or Doridin, methyprylon or Noludar, and flurazepam or Dalmane),* MAO inhibitors (e.g., Parnate, Marplan, Nardil), procarbazine, antacids, disulfiram (Antabuse)
Benzodiazepines (e.g., Librium, Valium)	Diphenylhydantoin (e.g., Dilantin), tricyclic antidepressants (amitriptyline, desipramine, doxepin, imipramine, nortriptyline, protriptyline, Elovil, Sinequan, Tofranil), ethyl alcohol (alcoholic beverages), barbiturates, other CNS depressants. Patient should avoid prolonged exposure to sunlight.
Coumarin anticoagulants	Phenylbutazone (e.g., Butazolidin),* oxyphenbutazone (Tandearil),* quinidine, quinine, salicylares (e.g., aspirin),* sulfonamides, thyroid preparations, glucagon, ethacrynic acid (Edecrin), tolbutamide, diphenylhydantoin (e.g., Dilantin), anabolic steroids,* chloral hydrate, clofibrate,* destrothyroxine,*

	indomethacin, disulfiram (Antabuse), antibiotics (particularly broad spectrum), estrogens, oral contraceptives with estrogens, barbiturates,* corticosteroids, ethchlorvynol, griseofulvin, flutethimide,* methylphenidate (Ritalin), cholestyramine
Digitalis glycosides	Injected calcium, glucose infusions, sympathomimetics, barbiturates, thiazides (e.g., Diuril, Esidrix), chlorthalidone (Hygroton), furosemide (Lasix), ethacrynic acid (Edecrin), succinylcholine, amphotericin B, propranolol (Inderal)
Diphenylhydantoin (e.g., Dilantin)	Coumarin anticoagulants,* corticosteroids, chloramphenicol, benzodiazepines (e.g., Librium, Valium), disulfiram (Antabuse),* isoniazid (INH),* methylphenidate (Ritalin), phenylbutazone (e.g., Butazolidin), sulfaphenazole, halothane, ethyl alcohol (alcoholic beverages)
Disulfiram (Antabuse)	Ethyl alcohol (not only alcoholic beverages but also any product containing alcohol, e.g., cough medicines, tonics),* barbiturates, diphenylhydantoin (e.g., Dilantin),* anticoagulants, metronidazole (Flagyl)
Guanethidine (Ismeline)	Ethyl alcohol (alcoholic beverages), propranolol (Inderal), methotrimeprazine,* amphetamines, ephedrine, methylphenidate (Ritalin), tricyclic antidepressants (amitriptyline, desipramine, doxepin, imipramine, nortriptyline, Elavil, Sinequan,

	Tofranil),* phenothiazines, diethylpropion, cocaine, procarbazine, other antihypertensives, diuretics
MAO inhibitors (e.g., Parnate, Marplan, Nardil)	Sympathomimetics (including amphetamines, anorexiants, and nonprescription cold and hay fever preparations containing vasoconstrictors),* general anesthetics,* all CNS depressants,* tricyclic antidepressants (amitriptyline, desipramine, doxepin, imipramine, nortriptyline, protriptyline, Elovil, Sinequan, Tofranil),* high-tyramine foods (e.g., cheese, sour cream, pickled herring, chicken livers, broad beans, chocolate, and yeast extracts), sulfonylureas (Orinase, Diabinese), insulin.
Methyldopa (Aldomet)	Methotrimeprazine, propranolol (Inderal), amphetamines, other anti-hypertensives, diuretics, procarbazine
Methylphenidate (Ritalin)	Tricyclic antidepressants (amitriptyline, desipramine, doxepin, imipramine, nortriptyline, protriptyline, Elovil, Sinequan, Tofranil), coumarin anticoagulants, diphenylhydantoin (e.g., Dilantin), primidone (Mysoline), phenylbutazone (e.g., Butazolidin), guanethidine (Ismeline), barbiturates
Narcotic analgesics	Neuromuscular block agents, ethyl alcohol (alcoholic beverages),* barbiturates,* other CNS depressants*
Penicillins	Probenecid (Benemid), tetracyclines, chloramphenicol, erythromycins, food, cephalosporins

Phenothiazines (e.g., Compazine, Thorazine, Stelazine)	Ethyl alcohol (alcoholic beverages), guanethidine (Ismelin), levodopa, quinidine, barbiturates, other CNS depressants
Phenylbutazone (e.g., Butazolidin)	Coumarin anticoagulants,* sulfonylureas (Orinase, Diabinese),* diphenylhydantoin (e.g., Dilantin), sulfonamides
Probenecid (Benemid)	Sulfonamides, sulfinpyrazone, penicillins, cephalosporins, nitrofurantoin, indomethacin, P.A.S.,* dapsone
Propranolol (Inderal)	Sulfonylureas (Orinase, Diabinese),* phenformin (DBI), insulin, anti-hypertensives, digitalis glycosides, isoproterenol, MAO inhibitors,* quinidine, guanethidine (Ismelin), anti-cholinergics (e.g., atropine), reserpine, tricyclic antidepressants (amitriptyline, desipramine, doxepin, imipramine, nortriptyline, protriptyline, Elovil, Sinequan, Tofranil)
Salicylates (e.g., aspirin)	Phenylbutazone (e.g., Butazolidin), oxyphenbutazone (Tandearil), P.A.S., coumarin anticoagulants,* sulfonylureas (Orinase, Diabinese), heparin, methotrexate, probenecid (Benemid),* spironolactone, sulfinpyrazone,* ethyl alcohol (alcoholic beverages)
Sulfisoxazole (e.g., gantrisin)	Aspirin, vitamin C
Sulfonamides	Sulfinpyrazone, probenecid (Benemid), PABA (sometimes included in nonprescription painkiller combinations),* phenylbutazone (e.g., Butazolidin), methenamine (e.g., Mandelamine), cholestyramine

Sulfonylureas (Orinase, Diabinese)	Thyroid replacement therapy, oral contraceptives with estrogens, ethyl alcohol (alcoholic beverages),* anabolic steroids, chloramphenicol, MAO inhibitors,* phenylbutazone (e.g., Butazolidin),* propranolol (Inderal),* salicylates (e.g., aspirin),* destrothyroxine,* corticosteroids, sulfonamides, acetazolamide, epinephrine, diuretics, coumarin anticoagulants, thiazides (e.g., Diuril, Esidrix)
Tetracylines	Antacids containing divalent or trivalentcations (e.g., Maalox, Mylanta, Gelusil, Tums, Alkaids),* milk and milk products,* methoxyflurane (inhalant anesthetic used in hospital),* food, sodium bicarbonate. Patient should avoid prolonged exposure to sunlight.
Thiazides (e.g., Diuril, Esidrix)	Corticosteroids, vasopressors (e.g., Norepinephrine), sulfonylureas (Orinase, Diabinese), phenformin, insulin, digitalis glycosides, gallamine, tubocurarine, anti-hypertensives, methotrexate
Tricyclic antidepressants (amitriptyline, desipramine, doxepin, imipramine, nortriptyline, protriptyline, Elovil, Sinequan, Tofranil)	Ethyl alcohol (alcoholic beverages),* benzodiazepines (e.g., Librium, Valium), ethchlorvynol (e.g., Placidyl), guanethidine (Ismelin),* CNS depressants, reserpine, sympathomimetics, vasodilators, disulfiram anticholinergics, (Antabuse),* propranolol (Inderal)

First Aid for Common Ills

Curing Hiccups

The following remedies all have advocates:
Swallowing dry 1 teaspoonful of ordinary white granulated sugar.
or
Swallowing 1 tablespoonful of vinegar.
or
Holding breath and controlling and calming diaphragm muscles.

Relieving Pain from a Bee Sting

Make a paste of ¼ teaspoon meat tenderizer from the supermarket plus 1 to 2 teaspoons water *or* by crushing a natural-papaya-enzyme tablet (from the health-food store) in a little water; dab the paste on the stung part.

Relieving the Itch from Gnat Bites

A few drops of lemon juice on the gnat bite should stop the itching.

▲Relieving Itching from Mosquito or Flea Bites and Poison Ivy

Apply hot water (120° to 130° F.) for a few seconds for relief up to three hours.
▲**Caution:** *Do not treat skin this way when poison ivy has raised blisters or there is extensive body surface affected by poison ivy. Children have very sensitive skin, so use hot water with care.*

Treatment for Ivy Poisoning

1 tablespoon sodium thiosulphate   2 cups water

Apply the solution to the affected part with pads of cotton 4 or 5 times a day and allow to dry on the skin. The blisters may be opened with a sterile needle; in this case, apply the solution before opening and immediately after.

Sunburn Lotion

After a cool (not ice-cold) bath, apply a paste made of equal amounts of baking soda and corn starch mixed with a little cool water.

▲ Wart Removers

Soak the affected part of the body in a solution of 1½ tablespoons table salt in ½ cup water, twice a day for several weeks; *or* apply a 10 percent solution of salicylic acid twice a day with a cotton-tipped applicator. The salicylic solution is made by dissolving 1 teaspoonful of salicylic acid in 9 teaspoons boiling water; store in a capped bottle.

▲ **Caution:** *Keep salicylic acid out of the reach of children.*

Part II.

The Foods You Eat

BREAD, CAKES, AND COOKIES
Additives in Bread

Unless the bread you buy is what the government considers a "specialty" bread—that is, if what you buy is white, enriched white, raisin, or whole-wheat bread and/or rolls—a great many of the ingredients do not need to be listed on the label. Even if a bread company does decide to list some ingredients on the label of these breads, there is no reason to suppose the company has listed *all* the ingredients—they are not required to. The phrase "no preservatives added" does not ensure that a number of other chemicals haven't been added—chemicals such as dough conditioners, bleaches, and emulsifiers. "Specialty" breads, on the other hand, must list everything.

Italian Bread Crumbs

Save leftover bread slices in a bag in the freezer until you have a good quantity. Then break the bread into small pieces and dry them in the oven (250° F.) on a cookie sheet until they are crisp but not brown. Put the pieces in a blender and crumb, *or* put them in a paper bag and crush them with a rolling pin.

To each 2 cups of the bread crumbs add ¼ teaspoon thyme, 1 teaspoon basil or oregano, and ¼ teaspoon garlic powder. If you like, add a dash of cayenne pepper or ½ teaspoon crushed dry red pepper. Store in a closed jar.

Biscuit Mix

8 cups flour 4 teaspoons salt
3 tablespoons and 2 teaspoons tartrate-type baking powder

Mix the flour, baking powder, and salt together and store in covered container.

To make 6 or 8 biscuits: Take 1 rounded cup of the biscuit mix; add 1 tablespoon cooking oil and ⅓ cup milk. Stir and beat lightly with a fork, just until the lumps are out. *Either* flour and roll out with your fingers and cut with a biscuit cutter, then bake on an ungreased cookie sheet; *or* do not flour and drop into greased muffin tins. Bake 12 to 15 minutes at 450° F.

Whole-Wheat Biscuit Mix

9 cups whole-wheat flour
2 cups nonfat dry milk
6 tablespoons baking powder

4 tablespoons sugar
1 teaspoon salt
1½ cups oil

Stir the dry ingredients together, mixing very well; add the oil and mix well until the oil disappears. Store in a covered container in the refrigerator—use within two months.

To make 15 biscuits: Put 3 cups of the mix in a bowl, add ⅔ cup water or a little less, and stir well. Knead the dough about 15 times, roll it to ½-inch thickness, and cut with a glass or biscuit cutter into 2-inch biscuits. Bake on a cookie sheet at 400° F. until brown, about 15 to 20 minutes.

Formula for Remembering the Order of Ingredients for Cookies and Cakes

According to Peg Bracken in the *I Hate to Housekeep Book*, one reluctant housekeeper remembers the sentence "Shirley shouldn't eat fresh mushrooms" to remind her that first one combines the shortening and sugar, then one adds the eggs, then flour, then milk (or other liquid).

Cake Mix

9 cups cake flour
   (sifted before measuring)
5 cups sugar

4 tablespoons baking powder
4 teaspoons salt

Mix the flour, baking powder, salt, and sugar together, and store in a covered container.

To make 1 cake (10-inch tube pan, two 8-inch layer pans, or 9-inch by 5-inch loaf pan): Do not butter the pans. Preheat the oven to 350° F. for tube or layer pans, to 325° F. for loaf pan. Put a scant 4 cups of the cake mix into a bowl and pour in ½ cup salad oil and ½ cup milk. Stir until the flour is dampened, then beat for 2 minutes. Add ½ cup milk, 2 eggs (or 5 egg yolks), and 1 teaspoon vanilla extract or 2 teaspoons grated lemon rind; beat another 2 minutes, and pour into the pans. If in layer pans, bake 30 minutes; in a tube or a loaf pan, bake about 55 minutes.

Oreo™ Style Cookie Filling

2 cups Crisco
2 cups confectioner's sugar (powdered sugar)
1 tablespoon unflavored gelatin
⅓ cup cold water

Soften the gelatin in the water. In a separate bowl, blend the Crisco and powdered sugar; add the gelatin water to the mixture.

CEREALS

Sugar in Commercial Dry Cereals

The Center for Science in the Public Interest has analyzed the sugar content of one brand of dry cereals—Kellogg—based on Kellogg's data:

Cereal	Sugar
All-Bran	14 percent
Apple Jacks	56 percent
Bran Buds	25 percent
Cocoa Krispies	46 percent
Concentrate	11 percent
Corn Flakes	7 percent
Country Morning	25 percent
Country Morning with raisins & dates	21 percent
40% Bran	18 percent
Froot Loops	53 percent
Frosted Mini-Wheats	28 percent
Frosted Rice	39 percent
Pep	14 percent
Product 19	11 percent
Raisin Bran	21 percent
Rice Krispies	11 percent
Special K	7 percent
Sugar Frosted Flakes	42 percent

Sugar Pops	39 percent
Sugar Smacks	56 percent

For comparison, one might note that soda pop contains 4.2 percent sugar, and a Milky Way candy bar, 26.8 percent.

Granola

3 cups oats
½ cup wheat germ
1 cup nuts, chopped
¼ cup sunflower seeds, chopped
¼ cup sesame seeds
½ cup raisins
¼ cup honey
¼ cup oil
¼ teaspoon vanilla extract

In a large bowl, put together the oats, wheat germ, nuts, sunflower seeds, sesame seeds, and raisins. In a small saucepan, heat the honey, oil, and vanilla; pour this liquid over the dry mixture and stir it up so that all the dry surfaces are coated. Spread the mixture thinly in shallow baking pans and bake at 325 F. for 15 to 20 minutes, or until it is lightly browned. Stir halfway through the baking time. Check to be sure the raisins don't burn. Store in a covered container. Serve the same way you serve any dry cereal—with milk and fresh fruit, or with yogurt or applesauce.

CHEESE

Chemical Additives in Cheese

CHEESE, PASTEURIZED PROCESS

This may contain any of 13 different chemicals, which the manufacturer is not required to show on the label, plus artificial coloring and flavoring.

CHEESE FOOD, PASTEURIZED PROCESS

This is pasteurized-process cheese with a dairy product such as milk or whey added. All the additives, artificial color and flavoring, preservatives, salt, and acidifying agents must be shown on the label.

CHEESE SPREAD, PASTEURIZED PROCESS

This is another pasteurized-process cheese with lots of additives—which are on the label.

Cold-pack Cheese, Club Cheese, or Comminuted Cheese

Like pasteurized-process cheese, each of these cheeses has lots of additives—the difference is that here there's no heat used in the processing.

Specific Cheeses and Their Additives

American Cheese

This is a misuse of the word "American," if you think of that word as connoting purity, naturalness, and straightforwardness. American cheese is a processed cheese that is filled with chemical additives that are not listed on the label, as well as artificial chemical coloring and flavoring.

Bel Paese

This cheese has no chemicals unless they're listed.

Blue or Bleu Cheese

This cheese may have blue or green coloring added that is not listed on the label. Danish imports, however, are unlikely to have these additives.

Brie

This cheese has no artificial coloring or preservatives.

Camembert

This cheese is made without chemicals.

Cheddar

This cheese may have artificial color added without its being listed on the label. It also may have other chemicals, but the others will be listed.

Cottage Cheese

This sometimes comes with additives that need not be mentioned on the label. Certain companies make cottage cheese that does not include these additives—Arden, Axelrod, Breakstone, Carnation, Friendship, Hood, Jerseymaid, and Tuttle.

Edam

Domestic Edam may have artificial color added without saying so on the label; imported Edam is free of artificial color. Other chemicals, if added, must be shown on the label.

Farmer Cheese

This cheese is without additives unless they're listed on the label.

Feta Cheese

This cheese has no chemical additives.

Gorgonzola

This, like blue cheese, may be colored without so stating on the label.

Gruyère

Very much like Swiss cheese in taste and texture, this cheese is made without artificial coloring and is made from milk that is not bleached with chemicals.

Limburger

This cheese is without chemical additives.

Monterey Jack

This cheese is made without chemicals unless they are listed on the label.

Mozzarella

This cheese is made without chemical additives, except for some "low moisture" mozzarellas; if they do have additives, they'll be listed on the label.

Muenster

This cheese is made without additives unless an additive is listed on the label.

Port-Salut

This cheese has no additives unless they are listed on the label.

Pot Cheese

This cheese is free of additives.

Provolone

This cheese may have added artificial coloring without so stating on the label.

Ricotta Cheese

This cheese is made without chemical additives unless they're listed on the label.

Romano

This cheese may have blue or green coloring added without its being stated on the label. The Italian imports are not likely to have this coloring added.

Roquefort Cheese

This cheese is made without artificial coloring or undesirable additives.

Swiss Cheese

This cheese may have artificial color added that is not listed on the label.

Cottage Cheese

4 quarts reconstituted nonfat dry milk	1 rennet tablet
¼ cup buttermilk	½ cup cream

Soak the rennet tablet in a little water to dissolve it. Begin to heat the milk and buttermilk; when it is lukewarm, add the rennet tablet and continue heating slowly. When it is 100° keep it at that temperature 30 minutes, then let it stand at room temperature 24 hours. Strain it through a cheesecloth or dishtowel, rinse the curds with cold water, then add the cream. If you do not wish to use cream, you can use the same amount of reconstituted nonfat dry milk made double or triple strength.

Spreads and a Dip

Basic Cheese Spread

½ cup milk
1 egg
½ teaspoon salt

¾ pound cheddar cheese
¼ teaspoon dry mustard

Beat the egg in a large bowl, then grate the cheese into the bowl, and add in mustard and salt. Heat the milk in a double boiler or in a saucepan at a very low temperature. Add the egg-and-cheese mixture to the milk and cook for 15 minutes, stirring occasionally. This will keep for a week or more in a covered jar in the refrigerator. For variety, you might want to stir in one of the following before storing the cheese spread: crumbled crisp bacon; 2 tablespoons chopped pimiento; ¼ teaspoon caraway seeds, sage, or other herbs; 1 clove of garlic, squeezed; 1 teaspoon fresh minced onion.

Cheese Spread from Stale Cheese

Stale cheese, pulverized in a meat-grinder or blender with a raw onion. Mustard (prepared or dry), olives (without pits), Worcestershire sauce, nutmeg, pickle, yogurt—any could be added.

Boursin Cheese Spread

½ cup cottage cheese
2 tablespoons butter
2 to 3 teaspoons salt

4 cloves garlic, crushed
4 tablespoons minced parsley

Squeeze all the liquid out of the cheese and mash it together with the butter until smooth. Stir in the garlic, the parsley, and the salt.

Cheddar Cheese Spread

3 cups or ¾ pound
    Cheddar cheese, grated
4 to 5 teaspoons yogurt

Pinch of cayenne pepper
¼ to ½ cup apple juice
¾ teaspoon nutmeg

Work together the cheese, yogurt, nutmeg, cayenne, and apple juice; make a stiff paste. Store in the refrigerator in covered containers.

Roquefort Cheese Dip

1 pound cottage cheese	1 tablespoon chives, chopped
¼ cup milk	1 tomato, chopped
1 to 2 teaspoons salt	2 ounces (or ½ cup) Roquefort cheese, crumbled

In a blender or food mill, mash and blend all ingredients until there are no more lumps. Good for dipping crackers or vegetables.

Storing Cheese

Plastic wrappers are needed to keep cheese from drying out in the refrigerator; *or* you can spread butter on the exposed surfaces.

COFFEE STRETCHERS AND COFFEE SUBSTITUTES

Chicory

1 part chicory   2 parts coffee

Mix chicory in the pot with the coffee and brew as usual.

Dandelion-Chicory-Cinnamon Drink

1 part roasted dandelion root   2 parts chicory
Dash of cinnamon

Mix, and enclose in a metal teaball; add hot water to brew as one brews tea.

Quantities in Commercial Packages

Commercial coffee—
   40 cups from 1 pound.

Commercial tea—
   240 cups from 1 pound.

EGGS

The Amount of Egg for Your Money

Size	Ounces per Dozen
extra-large	27 to 30
large	24 to 27
medium	21 to 24
small	18 to 21

If large eggs are more than 10 cents cheaper than extra-large, buy the large and you're getting more ounces of egg for your money. If medium are more than 7 cents cheaper than large, the medium will give you more egg for your money. The small eggs are rarely found in supermarkets; but if you can find them, they're sure to be a bargain.

Brown eggs and white eggs are the same on the inside. Don't pay a premium price for color.

Cooking Eggs in the Shell

If the shells tend to crack, add a spoonful of salt to the water.

Keeping Poached Eggs Intact

Add a teaspoon of vinegar to the water beforehand; then swirl the water and slip the egg gently into the center of the swirl. As soon as the first egg is sufficiently coagulated not to spread out into the water, swirl the water again and add the next egg.

FLOURS

Triple-Enriched All-Purpose Flour

In the bottom of a quart jar, place:

4 tablespoons soy flour
4 tablespoons nonfat dry milk
4 teaspoons wheat germ

Fill the rest of the jar with all-purpose enriched white flour or with whole-grain flour. Cover and store.

Enriched Cake Flour

In the bottom of each cup of flour called for, place 2 tablespoons corn starch; fill the cup with unsifted Triple-Enriched All-Purpose Flour.

Substituting Whole-Wheat Flour for White Flour

Use ¾ cup whole-wheat flour for each cup of white flour the recipe calls for. When measuring the whole-wheat flour, do not sift it, but stir it lightly. You'll need less oil, but more liquid: use 2 tablespoons of oil for each 3 tablespoons in the recipe; and add 1 or 2 tablespoons extra of water or milk when making a cake, and 2 to 3 extra tablespoons when making bread.

Baking Powder

Double-acting baking powder does not provide twice as much leavening but does provide leavening in two different stages. The other types, tartrate and phosphate baking powders, are also called "fast-acting." Several scientists have questioned the healthfulness of using double-acting baking powder because it includes aluminum salts. A sure-and-safe route would be to use tartrate or phosphate baking powders—that is, the "fast-acting" ones—and solve the fast-action problem by not adding the liquid ingredients to your recipe until just before you put it in the oven.

FRUITS AND FRUIT DRINKS

Applesauce

Canned or bottled fruits do not include additives that you cannot detect—their presence is always indicated on the label. Most canned fruits do include, though, a great deal of added sugar. If you buy applesauce, you pay for water, salt, extra acids, some kind of sugar, acid preservatives, coloring, spices, and artificial vitamin C—plus the jar, of course. With either a blender or a potato masher, even just a fork, you can make a much more nutritious applesauce yourself in just a few minutes. Core and dice your apples (peel them only if they're waxed), and either purée them raw in the blender *or* steam them, stirring now and then, in a saucepan over a medium flame (if you're cooking them, you might have to add a few spoonfuls of water at first; don't cook them more than a very few minutes, until they're barely soft). Add about 1 tablespoon lemon juice for each 4 or 5 apples, if they aren't tart; add a little sugar or honey if the apples are too tart, and shake in a little cinnamon and nutmeg.

Peeled and/or Sliced Peaches

In preparing peaches ahead of time, to prevent discoloration, immerse the peaches or peach slices in half milk, half hot water; rinse them before serving.

Fruit Drinks, Ades, and Nectars

Canned or bottled or frozen fruit drinks, fruit ades, fruit nectars, and fruit punches are not the healthiest beverages—a "juice drink" is only ½ juice, an "ade" is ¼ juice, and a "drink" is only ⅒ juice. All of them have sugar and water added, and almost all of them have artificial color, flavor, and preservatives. Look on the label. There are other chemical additives in most of them, too; these do not have to be listed on the label, and aren't. It's healthier to use real fruit juice and, if someone especially likes ades, to dilute and sweeten the juice yourself. Lemonade is made from the juice of one lemon, 1 to 2 tablespoons sugar, and ice cubes; fill the rest of the glass with water. For orangeade, combine 2 cups orange juice, ½ cup lemon juice, ½ cup honey, and 1 cup water; serve over ice.

Rose Hip Juice

1 cup rose hips   2 tablespoons lemon juice

As soon as the rose hips have been gathered, chill them in the refrigerator. After chilling, remove the stem and blossom ends; add the hips to 1½ cups boiling water in a nonmetal pot, simmer 15 minutes, then let stand at room temperature 24 hours. Strain; then bring the juice to a full rolling boil, add the lemon juice. Put up in a sterilized jar and seal.

For jelly add pectin, bring to a boil, add sugar to taste, bring to a high boil for a minute, take off the froth, and put up in sterilized jars.

WINE MAKING

Dandelion Wine

4 pounds sugar	1 gallon dandelion flowers
Peels of 2 oranges	Juices of the dandelions
Peel of 1 lemon	(squeezings from the stems)
1 ounce yeast	

Boil the sugar in 1 gallon water until dissolved; then pour, still boiling, over the orange and lemon peels in a crock. When the mixture has cooled to lukewarm, add the dandelion flowers, the dandelion juice, and the yeast. Cover the crock and let it sit for 10 days, stirring daily, and taking out any flowers that have gone bad. Then strain it through cheesecloth into a clean receptacle. Keep it in a warm room, with two layers of cotton tied over the top, as long as bubbles are rising. When it is quiet, begin "clearing." Siphon off the liquid, leaving the yeast deposits, cover tightly, and set in a cool room for several weeks. Siphon again, and continue the process until the wine is clear—which may take three months.

Use old wine or cognac bottles with indentations in the bottom; sterilize the bottles, adding soda to the sterilizing water, then rinse them and dry them in a warm oven. Put two raisins in each bottle before filling. Plug them with corks, wire the corks, and store the bottles on their sides for 6 months to let it age in a cool, dark place.

Concord Wine

4 12-ounce cans frozen concentrated grape juice	1 ounce dry yeast
1 pound sugar	2 oranges, quartered
	2 lemons, quartered

In a kettle, heat the juice and water to boiling. Turn off the flame, add the other ingredients—sprinkle the yeast across the top—then spread two thicknesses of clean old sheeting over the top of the kettle, fastened with string or elastic. Put the lid on to keep out dust. After 9 to 14 days the fermentation will stop and the yeast will fall to the bottom. Siphon off the liquid, transferring it to another container, and let it sit for several weeks; repeat the siphoning twice more, at several-week intervals, until the wine is free of sediment. Transfer the clear wine into old wine or cognac bottles, sterilize, cork, and store as in the Dandelion Wine recipe. This wine will not need aging.

HERBS AND SEASONINGS

Preserving Fresh Herbs

Preserve fresh herbs between layers of coarse salt (such as kosher salt), in tightly covered containers in the refrigerator. Put only one type herb in each container. Rinse the herbs before using. Herbs should keep this way for about two months and have better flavor than dried or frozen herbs.

Homemade Mustard

½ cup mustard seed
1 tablespoon chopped parsley
1 teaspoon chopped chervil
1 tablespoon chopped tarragon
1 tablespoon oil
1 tablespoon vinegar

Pulverize the mustard seed in a mortar, put it through a sieve; to the powder add the parsley, tarragon, chervil, oil, and vinegar. Use within a day or two; keep refrigerated. Black mustard seeds are stronger tasting than the other kinds.

JELLIES, GELATINS, AND BUTTERS

Additives in Jellies and Jams

Jellies and jams in the supermarket most often include chemical acid salts, manufactured from fungi, and chemical antifoaming agents—neither of which is mentioned on the label. Only the preservative and any flavoring or coloring agents are shown on the label.

The government specifies that there must be at least 45 percent fruit in jams and jellies—in most brands, the majority of what's in the jar is sugar, not fruit. Homemade spreads are healthier, and not that difficult to make. Write to the Superintendent of Documents, Government Printing Office, Washington, D.C., 20402, for the government pamphlet on making jams and jellies at home.

Of course, if you have raw fruit on hand, it can be combined with a little sugar (and sometimes lemon juice) and crushed, making an excellent instant spread.

Gelatin Desserts

Commercial gelatin desserts, such as Jell-O, are mostly sugar—about 85 percent sugar—with some gelatin. Very often, all the flavoring, color, and acid are manufactured chemicals. Making your own gelatin dessert is both healthy and easy. Sprinkle 1 envelope gelatin (1 tablespoon) evenly over ½ cup cold fruit juice in a small saucepan. Over low heat, stir until the gelatin dissolves (2 or 3 minutes). Take it off the flame, add 1½ cups more fruit juice and ¼ cup sugar; pour the mixture into 4 dishes or into a serving bowl and chill 2 to 4 hours, until it's firm. If you're going to add solid fruits, do it when the gel is slightly thickened, then put it back in the refrigerator. (Either fresh or canned juices and fruits can be used, with the exception of pineapple—fresh pineapple will prevent the gel from thickening, so pineapple in gelatin must be canned.)

Apple Butter

1 quart sweet apple cider *or* unsweetened apple juice	4 quarts tart eating apples (such as Macintosh) quartered

When you quarter the apples, remove the cores but not the peels. Boil the cider or juice to reduce it by half; meantime, put the apples through the blender or chopper until the skins are in tiny pieces. Add the apples to the reduced cider and simmer, uncovered, until the mixture is the consistency of marmalade. You may wish to add up to 2 tablespoons of lemon juice and 1 tablespoon of cinnamon at the end.

Peanut Butter

2 cups peanuts, shelled	½ teaspoon salt
Up to ¼ cup safflower oil	1 teaspoon honey

In a blender or a meat grinder, pulverize the nutmeats—they should turn into a powder. Add the oil a little at a time, working it in, until you reach the consistency you like. Stir in the salt and honey; store in a covered container in the refrigerator. If, when you are about to use it, the oil has separated from the peanut butter, simply stir with the same knife you'll use to spread it.

Butters can be made from other nuts and seeds too—pecans, walnuts, sesame, sunflower, pumpkin.

MEAT, POULTRY, AND FISH

Prepared Meat Products

The federal government requires the following minimum amounts of meat from food packagers:

12 percent in frozen lasagna
25 percent in canned chili con carne
25 percent uncooked meat or 18 percent cooked meat in frozen meat casseroles
25 percent meat in frozen meat pies
30 percent meat in frozen entrees of meat with gravy and one vegetable
50 percent meat in canned beef with barbecue sauce
50 percent meatballs (containing no more than 12 percent extenders) in canned meatballs in sauce
35 percent meatballs (containing extenders) in canned spaghetti sauce with meatballs
40 percent breaded meat in frozen veal parmigiana

Lecithin

Use lecithin, a pure vegetable substance available in liquid form from natural-food stores, instead of Pam, which is the same thing in a spray can.

Meat Tenderizer

Instead of the meat tenderizers sold in supermarkets, an excellent butcher of my acquaintance recommends marinating meat in lemon juice.

Storing Meat

Fresh Meats	Days in 35° to 40° F. Refrigerator	Months in 0° F. Freezer
Variety meats	1–2	1
Ground meats, stew meats	1–2	2–3
Lamb and pork chops	3–5	3–4
Pork and veal roasts	3–5	4–8
Beef and lamb roasts	3–5	8–12
Beef steaks	3–5	8–12
Processed Meats		
Luncheon meats	3–5	0
Smoked sausage	7	0
Dry sausage	14–21	0
Frankfurters	7	½
Whole ham	7	1–2
Half ham	3–5	1–2
Ham slices	3	1–2
Cooked Meats	1–2	2–3
Fresh Poultry		
Giblets	1–2	3
Duck, goose, and turkey	1–2	6
Chicken	1–2	12
Cooked Poultry		
Pieces not covered with broth	1–2	1
Fried chicken	1–2	3
Pieces covered with broth	1–2	6

As a general rule-of-finger, if a piece of meat feels slimy, it's bad—throw it out.

Proteins without Meat

The following food combinations provide, when eaten in the same meal, the complete range of the amino acids that make up necessary protein:

rice with beans
or
rice with nuts and sesame seeds
or
whole-grain breads with nuts or beans
or
cornmeal with beans

Hamburgers

HAMBURGERS ON DEMAND

Shape ground beef into patties, wrap with aluminum foil, and freeze. They can be cooked one or more at a time whenever they are wanted.

HAMBURGER STRETCHER

Grate a raw potato into each pound of hamburger.

HAMBURGER FLAVORINGS

Inexpensive ground beef can be made more flavorful by mixing in any or all of the following: Worcestershire sauce, chopped onion, crushed garlic, salt, pepper, nutmeg, dry mustard. Flavored beef can be shaped in patties and frozen, or used immediately.

Meat Sauces

BARBECUE SAUCE

Most commercial barbecue sauce is loaded with chemicals—for flavor, color, and preservation—and sugar. You can instantly make your own with 1 cup each of vinegar, mustard, and molasses. For variety, you could add 1 cup chopped raw tomato and a couple of dashes of cayenne pepper; *or* add ¼ teaspoon each of tarragon, coriander, basil, and rosemary; *or*

½ cup each of catsup and oil and ¼ cup soy sauce plus 1 teaspoon hot pepper sauce.

Spaghetti Sauce with Meat (5 pints)

4 pounds lean ground beef	1 teaspoon to 1 tablespoon salt
4 medium onions, chopped	½ teaspoon pepper
1 cup celery, chopped	1 tablespoon oregano
3 6-ounce cans tomato paste	1 tablespoon basil
2 large cloves garlic, minced	

In a heavy saucepan, heat the meat, stirring it until it is browned. Add the rest of the ingredients with 3 cups water and simmer, uncovered, 1 hour—until the sauce is thick. After cooling, this can be frozen in convenient-size portions.

Sloppy Joes

2 cups Spaghetti Sauce with Meat (above)	1 teaspoon Worcestershire sauce
Hot pepper sauce, to taste	

Combine these ingredients; serve over buns.

Chili

2 cups Spaghetti Sauce with Meat (above)	1 15-ounce can kidney beans
	1 tablespoon chili powder

Combine these ingredients; serve in bowls or on plates, according to how thick you've made the Spaghetti Sauce with Meat.

Steak Sauces and Browning Aids

To avoid artificial coloring, artificial flavoring, and stabilizers, use only Lea & Perrins Worcestershire Sauce or pure soy sauce in place of any other commercial browning aids and steak sauces.

Sausages

Sausages that are inexpensive, delicious, fresh, and—to your own certain knowledge—free of chemical additives, preservatives, and artificial colorings are also easy to make.

Simple Sausage

2 pounds pork tenderloin
½ pound veal
1½ pounds fresh pork fat
2 cups rolled oats

1 tablespoon salt
1 teaspoon caraway seeds
⅛ teaspoon allspice
⅛ teaspoon ginger

Chop into ¼-inch dice the pork tenderloin, veal, and pork fat. Bring the rolled oats to a boil in 1 cup water; drain them immediately; cool, in refrigerator, 15 minutes. Meantime, grind, mix meat and fat with the oats, caraway seeds, allspice, ginger, and salt; form into patties. To store, wrap in aluminum foil and refrigerate. Cook in a skillet, browning well on both sides—add a little cooking oil if needed. This is a mild sausage suitable for any meal.

Gruetzwurst

4 pounds pork shoulder, cut in 1-inch pieces
2 pounds ground beef
3 cups rolled oats
3 onions, chopped

2 tablespoons butter
1 tablespoon sage
¼ teaspoon allspice
salt
pepper

Cook the pork shoulder and ground beef in water to cover, until they are tender. Meantime, cook the rolled oats (according to package directions) until thick; and cook the onions in the butter until the onions are transparent.

Dice the meat into ¼-inch pieces or grind coarsely in a meat grinder; combine with the oatmeal and onions, mix; then mix in sage, allspice, salt, and pepper. Form into patties. To store, wrap each patty in plastic wrapping and heat-seal with an iron, *being careful not to breathe the fumes;* put the wrapped patties in a deep kettle, add water to cover, and simmer, covered, 40 minutes. Transfer quickly to the refrigerator or freezer (this is one of the few sausages that can be stored several days in a freezer) for storage. The patties can be eaten cold or reheated in water.

Swedish Sausage

8 large potatoes
2 pounds round steak
2 pounds pork shoulder

1½ teaspoons dry mustard
¼ teaspoon nutmeg
1 tablespoon salt

2 medium onions, peeled
¼ teaspoon allspice, ground
½ teaspoon pepper
1 tablespoon allspice, whole

Peel and boil the potatoes; let them cool. Meantime, grind the round steak and pork shoulder with the fine disk in the meat grinder three times; or mince fine.

Chop the potatoes and onions finely, or put through the meat grinder, using the fine disk. Mix together the potatoes, onions, meat, allspice, dry mustard, nutmeg, salt, and pepper—add cold water to soften. Knead mixture with your hands.

At this point fry a little of the mixture to see if the taste is what you want. Add more seasonings if desired.

Stuff the mixture loosely into 2-foot-long natural casings, following the directions for soaking and rinsing casings that you'll get where you buy the casings. Tie the ends of the casings to form rings of each two. Refrigerate. To cook, boil 45 minutes—with the whole allspice added to the cooking water. As froth accumulates, remove it. Cut the sausage into 2-inch slices and serve hot or cold.

BREAKFAST SAUSAGES

2½ pounds lean pork
1½ teaspoons marjoram
¼ teaspoon nutmeg
2 teaspoons pepper
2½ teaspoons sage
½ teaspoon savory
2 teaspoons salt

Grind the pork coarsely in a meat grinder or dice it into ¼-inch pieces. Mix the marjoram, nutmeg, sage, savory, salt, and pepper together in ¼ cup warm water, then knead the spice mixture into the pork. Shape into patties. To store, wrap each patty in aluminum foil and refrigerate. To cook, brown patties on both sides—add a little oil to the pan if needed.

ITALIAN SAUSAGE

2½ pounds lean pork
½ pound lean beef
1 pound fresh pork fat
10 large cloves garlic, peeled and minced
2 teaspoons red pepper, crushed
2 teaspoons fennel seed, crushed
4 bay leaves, crumbled
1 teaspoon thyme
2 teaspoons salt
1 tablespoon whole black pepper
¼ teaspoon nutmeg
5 tablespoons salt

Grind the lean pork and the beef with the coarse blade in a meat grinder, or dice into ¼-inch pieces. Combine all the ingredients and work them together with a wooden spoon; shape into patties. To store, wrap each patty in aluminum foil and refrigerate. To cook, brown the patties on both sides—add a little oil to the pan if needed.

Chicken

Shake-and-Fry Chicken

For each 3 pounds of chicken pieces, put the following in a medium-size paper bag: ½ cup flour, ½ teaspoon pepper, 1 teaspoon salt, ½ teaspoon herbs of your choice (perhaps chervil, coriander, or nutmeg). Shake the bag. Then add the pieces of chicken to the bag, a few at a time, and shake to coat the chicken pieces; place the coated pieces in ½ to 1 inch oil in a hot skillet, cover and cook over medium heat 45 minutes to 1 hour. Turn the chicken pieces halfway through the cooking time.

Shake-and-Bake Style Chicken

Follow the recipe for Shake-and-Fry Chicken (above), but dip the chicken pieces in milk or water before shaking them in the paper bag; and instead of frying them, put them in a baking dish and drip a little oil on each piece. Bake at 350° F. for 45 minutes to 1 hour, turning halfway through and at that time dripping on a little more oil.

Colonel Sanders' Style Kentucky Fried Chicken

3 pounds fryer parts,
  cut small
2 packages Italian salad
  dressing mix (Good Seasons
  brand)
3 tablespoons flour
2 teaspoons salt
¼ cup lemon juice
2 tablespooons butter, softened
1½ pints salad oil
1 cup milk
1½ cups pancake mix,
  combined with: ½ teaspoon sage
  and ¼ teaspoon pepper

Wipe the chicken pieces dry. Make a paste of the salad dressing mix, flour, salt, lemon juice, and butter, and brush the paste on the chicken, coating the pieces evenly. Cover and refrigerate for several hours.

1½ hours before serving, heat ½ inch oil in 2 large skillets. Dip the chicken pieces in the milk, then in the pancake mix, coating them well. Dust off excess. Lightly brown the chicken—about 4 minutes for each side. Place them in one layer in shallow pans that are ovenproof. Spoon most of the remaining milk over the chicken, seal with foil, and bake 1 hour at 350° F. Uncover and bake 10 minutes at 400° (to crisp); baste again with milk.

Fish

Fried Fish in the Oven

Dip pieces of fish into milk that has been seasoned with your favorite herb (perhaps basil or tarragon), then roll them in fine bread crumbs. Place them in a single layer on a greased baking dish, drip a small amount of oil on each piece (approximately 2 tablespoons oil for each pound of fish), sprinkle with a little paprika for color, and bake at 500° F. for 10 to 15 minutes.

Arthur Treacher's Style Fish & Chips

3 pounds fish fillets
Buttermilk
1 lemon
1½ pints oil, for deep frying
White flour
2 cups pancake mix
2½ cups club soda

Soak the fish fillets in just enough buttermilk to cover them, slice the lemon over it, cover and refrigerate 2 to 3 hours.

In a heavy 2½-quart saucepan, heat the oil. Drain the milk from the fish, discarding milk and lemon. Cut the fish fillets in half, making triangles; dredge the triangles with flour.

In a separate container, mix the pancake mix and club soda—you want the consistency of buttermilk. Dip the floured fish pieces in the batter, let excess batter drip back into the bowl, and deep-fry the fish pieces 4 minutes each side. Keep warm in a 250° F. oven, without heaping, until all the pieces are fried.

MILK AND MILK PRODUCTS

Flavored Milk

CHOCOLATE MILK

Chocolate milk is not a good idea. One of the prime nutrients in milk is calcium, the bone and tooth builder, and chocolate cuts down on the body's ability to use calcium. For some good-tasting flavored milks, try any of the recipes that follow.

VANILLA MILK

¼ teaspoon vanilla extract and 1 teaspoon honey in a cup of milk.

PEANUT MILK

3 tablespoons peanut butter and 2 tablespoons honey in 4 cups milk. Mix with a rotary beater or blender until smooth; stir again before serving.

MOLASSES MILK

1 tablespoon molasses in 1 cup of milk.

BANANA MILK

½ banana, crushed with a fork, and 1 tablespoon molasses in a cup of milk.

HOT WHEAT MILK

¾ cup milk, 1 rounded teaspoon wheat germ, 1 teaspoon honey. Heat in a saucepan over low flame, with a stick of cinnamon. Take it off the stove before the mixture boils.

DATE-NUT MILK

¼ cup almonds, made into a powder in the blender; then add 3 pitted dates and ¾ cup milk and continue blending until smooth.

TOMATO MILK

¾ cup tomato juice, 1 egg, ⅛ teaspoon pepper sauce, ⅛ teaspoon salt,

2 tablespoons nonfat dry milk. Blend in the blender until thoroughly mixed.

Carrot-Orange Milk

Put ¾ cup orange juice and 1 small sliced carrot into the blender; blend until it's liquid. Add ½ banana, sliced, ⅓ cup nonfat dry milk, and 1 teaspoon honey; blend until smooth.

Seattle Delight

1 cup milk, ⅓ cup orange juice, 1 teaspoon honey, 1 sliced banana. Combine in a blender. This has the consistency of a Western milkshake.

Instant Breakfasts in a Blender
(Or with a fork or egg beater)

1 cup milk	1 teaspoon honey
2 tablespoons peanut butter	Fresh or dried fruit

or

1 cup milk	Pinch of cinnamon
½ teaspoon honey	Pinch of nutmeg

or

1 cup milk	1 tablespoon molasses

or

1 cup milk	1½ teaspoons honey
1 teaspoon unsweetened cocoa powder	

or

1 cup milk	Honey to taste
½ cup fresh or cooked or dried fruit	

or

¾ cup milk	1 tablespoon honey
½ large (or 1 small) banana	

or

1 cup milk	½ cup prune juice
4 pitted cooked prunes	1 teaspoon honey

Super-Strength Breakfast

Beat or blend together ½ cup each orange juice and milk, 1 or 2 tablespoons brewer's yeast or wheat germ, 1 tablespoon safflower oil, 2 tablespoons dry milk powder, and ½ teaspoon vanilla extract (or 1 teaspoon honey).

Milk Substitute

For those who cannot drink milk, a nutritious and good-tasting drink is nut "milk": Grind 1 cup nuts (peanuts, blanched almonds, or raw cashews) in a blender until powdery. Add 2 cups water in the blender and keep the motor on until the mixture is smooth. Stir in 2 teaspoons honey. More water can be stirred in to thin the "milk," if wanted.

Additives in Canned Milk

Evaporated Milk

Several chemical stabilizers may have been added that are not mentioned on the label. Carrageenan, a seaweed derivative treated with sulfur dioxide and alkali, is the only additive that government requires manufacturers to list on the label.

Sweetened Condensed Milk

There are no additives in this except for sweetener—40 percent sweetener—either sucrose, dextrose, or corn syrup.

Whipped Cream

Making Cream Whip Faster

Add a pinch of salt to the cream to increase the whipping speed.

Whipped "Cream" from Nonfat Dry Milk

½ cup nonfat dry milk
½ cup ice water
2 tablespoons orange juice
2 tablespoons honey *or* maple syrup *or* sugar

In a chilled bowl, put the dry milk and the ice water; beat with a rotary beater until the soft-peak stage (about 5 minutes). Add the orange juice and sweetening and continue to beat until it is fluffy (5 minutes or so more). Refrigerate. Use within 2 hours.

Yogurt

Yogurt in a Frying Pan

1 quart milk	3 tablespoons yogurt

Mix the milk and yogurt and divide into small containers (1- or 2-cup containers). Heat electric frying pan to 100° F.; fill it with ½ inch of hot tap water and put the yogurt dishes in the water. Cover the fry pan and let the yogurt ripen for 3 to 6 hours, or until it is thickened. Store in the refrigerator.

After the yogurt is ready, you may want to add flavoring—fresh fruit, perhaps crushed, with or without sugar and your choice of spices. A spoonful of jelly or jam can be added to an individual serving.

Yogurt on a Pilot Light

Fill a quart jar halfway up with non-fat powdered milk; add 2 or 3 tablespoons yogurt; add lukewarm water, stirring with a fork, until the jar is full. Cover the top with wax paper, then screw on the lid (no metal should be exposed to the mix while it's setting); wrap a bathtowel around the sides and top to trap the heat, and set the jar on the stove above the pilot light. Leave it for up to 10 hours, or until it looks like yogurt—check it after a few hours, and don't let it get overdone. Store in the refrigerator. May be flavored as above.

Yogurt Popsicles (8 servings)

2 cups yogurt	1 cup fresh mashed *or*
2 tablespoons corn syrup	blended *or* grated fruit
1 tablespoon honey	⅛ teaspoon nutmeg

Freeze the yogurt until it is half firm, then take it out and beat it well with the other ingredients. Return the mixture to the freezer in 8 popsicle molds or paper cups, or in an ice-cube tray. Freeze until firm.

Yogurt Sherbet (4 servings)

2 cups yogurt
Honey, to taste
2 cups fresh mashed *or* blended *or* grated fruit

Freeze the yogurt until it is the consistency of sherbet; take it out, beat it with the fruit, and refreeze.

PANCAKES

Pancakes, after they're cooked, can be frozen. Stack them with waxed paper or aluminum foil between each pancake, and wrap the stack in heavy plastic or foil; then take as many as you want at breakfast time and heat them in the toaster.

Pancake Mixes

Basic Pancake Mix

8 cups flour
5 tablespoons and 1 teaspoon baking powder
1 cup sugar
4 teaspoons salt

Mix the flour, baking powder, sugar, and salt, and store in a covered container.

To make 6 to 8 pancakes: In a bowl, mix 1 egg, 2 to 4 tablespoons melted butter, and ½ cup milk. Beat lightly. Add, all at once, a rounded cupful of the pancake mix to the milk mixture.

Whole-Wheat Pancake Mix #1

8 cups whole-wheat flour
1 teaspoon salt
2 cups dry non-fat milk
8 teaspoons baking powder
5 tablespoons brown sugar

Mix the ingredients and store them.

When you want to make pancakes: add sufficient warm water (and melted butter, if you like) to make whatever quantity of the mixture you're using into a thin batter; then cook on a hot, oiled griddle. These pancakes are best if they're small—3 or 4 inches in diameter.

Whole-Wheat Pancake Mix #2

6 cups whole-wheat flour
5 tablespoons plus 1 teaspoon baking powder
4 teaspoons salt
8 tablespoons sugar

Mix and store in a covered container.

To make 10 pancakes: Put a scant cup of the mix into a mixing bowl and add 1 cup milk, 1 egg, and 1½ tablespoons melted butter; stir until the dry ingredients are moistened.

Pancake Syrups and Topping

½ cup each molasses and honey, ½ teaspoon vanilla, and a pinch of salt. Heat.

or

2 cups sugar and ¾ cup water and ½ teaspoon vanilla. Heat.

or

½ cup butter, 1 cup honey, and 6 tablespoons (half a 6-ounce can) frozen orange juice, all at room temperature and beaten together.

or

¾ cup molasses and ⅓ cup butter. Heat.

SALAD DRESSINGS

Bottled Dressings and Mayonnaise

Salad dressings that contain "vegetable oil" usually include cottonseed oil. Cotton is not grown for eating and is sprayed with heavy amounts of noxious chemicals; thus, many nutrition specialists strongly advise against humans' taking cottonseed oil into their systems. Many commercial salad dressings also contain a preservative that has been linked to kidney damage.

All the common brands of mayonnaise use sugar as well as cottonseed oil, plus a chemical to keep the oil from crystallizing.

Basic Oil and Vinegar Dressing

¼ cup rice wine vinegar
¾ cup light Spanish olive oil

These two alone make a light and delicate, flavorful dressing; you can vary the flavor and make a vinaigrette-mustard dressing by adding

½ teaspoon dry mustard
½ teaspoon salt
¼ teaspoon freshly ground pepper

Vary things further by adding to the vinaigrette-mustard dressing 1 clove of crushed garlic. Or add the garlic plus 1 or 2 tablespoons fresh herbs *or* ½ teaspoon dried herbs. Or add 3 tablespoons grated Parmesan cheese. Or mash a hard-cooked egg yolk into the vinaigrette-mustard dressing.

You can vary the basic oil and vinegar dressing by adding 3 tablespoons of Roquefort cheese, crumbled; *or* add ½ teaspoon curry powder and a pinch of ginger, plus raisins and 1 teaspoon minced onion; *or* add ¼ teaspoon each basil and oregano with some minced fresh parsley and 1 crushed garlic clove. On a fruit salad, ½ teaspoon crushed coriander seed, added to the oil and vinegar, is different and delicious; for cold cooked or raw vegetable salad, marinate in the oil and vinegar with 2 tablespoons fresh chopped (or ½ teaspoon dried) dill.

Basic Mayonnaise (About 2 cups)

2 egg yolks
½ teaspoon salt
1 teaspoon dry mustard
Pinch of cayenne pepper
¼ cup vinegar
1 cup olive oil
1 cup salad oil

Beat the egg yolks until they're thick and lemon-colored; add the salt, mustard, cayenne, and half the vinegar; beat the mixture well. Mix the two oils together in a separate container, then add them to the mixture while continuing to beat the mixture. Add the oils a drop at a time at first, then increase the speed at which you add the oils as the mixture becomes thicker. Finally, add the rest of the vinegar; beat well again. (Some people leave out ¼ cup of the oil until the last because, if the mayonnaise separates, it will be cured when you put in the last of the oil.)

Mayonnaise Made in a Blender (About 1½ cups)

Juice of 1 lemon
½ teaspoon dry mustard
½ teaspoon salt

1 egg
1 cup olive oil

Put all the ingredients except ¾ cup of the olive oil into the container of an electric blender. Put on the cover; turn the blender on to low, then immediately remove the cover and add the ¾ cup olive oil in a small, steady stream.

French Dressings

French Dressing Mix (8 cups)

2 to 4 teaspoons salt
4 teaspoons paprika

4 teaspoons dry mustard
½ teaspoon black pepper

Mix these ingredients; keep them stored at room temperature in a tightly covered jar.

For 1 cup French dressing, mix 1 tablespoon of French Dressing Mix with ¼ cup vinegar *or* lemon juice and ¾ cup salad oil.

Garlic French Dressing (1 cup)

1 tablespoon French Dressing Mix (above)
1 garlic clove, crushed

¼ cup vinegar *or* lemon juice

Curry French Dressing (1 cup)

1 tablespoon French Dressing Mix (above)
¼ to ½ teaspoon curry powder

¼ cup vinegar *or* lemon juice
¾ cup salad oil

Roquefort Dressing (1⅞ cup)

1 tablespoon French Dressing Mix (above)
2 teaspoons water

¾ cup crumbled Roquefort cheese
¼ cup vinegar *or* lemon juice
¾ cup salad oil

VEGETABLES, PASTA, AND RICE

Canned and Frozen Vegetables

Frozen potatoes, carrots, and beets—the root vegetables—are treated by food processors to make peeling easier; one of the methods is a caustic lye bath, which destroys vitamins and minerals. Potatoes are further treated with a number of chemicals—one author compares them to embalming fluid—so they won't darken, as they normally do on exposure to light.

Commercial canning of vegetables often relies on the addition of chemicals and heat that are highly destructive of the vitamins and other nutrients in fresh vegetables. In fact, often the greatest amount of nutrition is in the liquid in the can, not in the vegetable; and the liquid generally is discarded when you use the vegetables. Two exceptions are canned pimientos and canned tomatoes that are packed in their own liquid.

Vegetable Shortening

Vegetable shortening that comes in a can is hydrogenated, or saturated, and there are chemical emulsifiers, bleaches, colors, preservatives, and stabilizers added. Use oil or softened butter instead, in order to avoid these chemicals.

Vegetable Soufflés

1 to 2 cups cooked and minced, puréed or riced vegetables	2 to 3 tablespoons butter
	2 to 3 tablespoons flour
	1 cup warm milk
3 to 4 eggs	

Separate eggs and, in their separate bowls, let them come to room temperature. In a saucepan, over low heat, melt the butter, add the flour, and whisk it until there are no undissolved lumps. Add the warm milk a little at a time, whisking constantly; allow this sauce to continue cooking on the lowest of flames, stirring it frequently, while you prepare the other food.

Preheat the oven to 350° F. Heat the vegetable in whatever seasonings you prefer (salt, pepper, onion, garlic, herbs, spices—whatever is good with that vegetable). While this is heating, beat the egg yolks with a fork or whisk until they are lemon yellow. As you continue to beat the yolks, add 4 spoonfuls of the heated vegetable, one spoonful at a time; then combine all the vegetables with the egg yolks, stir in the white sauce from the pot on the stove, and set aside.

Beat the egg whites stiff but not dry. Fold them into the vegetable mixture—use a light touch, don't mash or stir the egg whites. Pour into a buttered 1½ quart baking dish, preferably one with straight up-and-down sides, and bake 30 minutes. Serve immediately.

Growing Sprouts for Salads

Excellent sources of protein and vitamins, sprouts can be grown in a jar in 3 to 6 days, and eaten fresh in a salad or cooked. Put seeds in a glass jar (remember that sprouts can grow to eight or ten times the volume of the seeds) and cover the jar with muslin fastened with a rubber band. Fill the jar, through the muslin, with water; shake well, then drain off the water. Lay the jar down on its side. Water the seeds this way each morning and evening until the sprouts have grown as much as you want them to.

Seed	Days to Sprout
Alfalfa	4–6
Alphatoco	3–5
Fenugreek	3–6
Lentils	3–6
Mung bean	3–5
Soya bean	4–6
Triticale	3–6

Sprouted seeds and beans have more protein, vitamin B, and vitamin C—and fewer calories—pound for pound, then they had when they were unsprouted. For instance, ¼ pound of soybeans provides 457 calories, 38.7 grams of protein, 80 units of vitamin A, 1.25 milligrams thiamine, .36 milligrams of riboflavin, 2.5 milligrams of niacin, and a negligible amount of vitamin C. That ¼ pound of soybeans will grow about 1 pound of bean sprouts—which will provide 209 calories, 68.1 grams of protein, 360 units of vitamin A, 1.03 milligrams thiamine, .88 milligrams riboflavin, 3.9 milligrams niacin, and 58 milligrams of vitamin C.

Green Tomato Relish

2 quarts cut-up green tomatoes
⅔ cup salt
1½ teaspoons *each* of pepper, mustard, cinnamon cloves, and allspice
⅓ cup white mustard seed
2 or 3 onions, chopped
1 quart vinegar

Cover the cut-up tomatoes with the salt and let them stand for a day. Add the other ingredients, boil it all for 15 minutes, and put it up in sterilized jars.

Pasta

Whole-Wheat Eggless Noodles

3 cups whole-wheat flour
2 cups yogurt
2 teaspoons salt

Mix the ingredients to make a stiff dough, and squeeze and knead it 2 to 3 minutes. Roll it out to a thin layer on a floured board. Let it stay there for 5 minutes, then cut it into ¼ inch slices; spread the slices out on paper and let them dry at room temperature until they are hard—several hours. Store in a closed container. *Or*, cook them right away, without waiting for them to dry. Cook in boiling, salted water, about 10 minutes.

Whole-Wheat Egg Barley

4 cups whole-wheat flour
1 teaspoon salt
4 eggs

Blend the ingredients and 5 tablespoons water with your hands and knead the dough until it is very stiff—5 minutes. Divide dough into small batches. Flatten each batch a little, and allow it to become partly dry—about 1 hour. Rub each lump against a coarse grater to make pea-size pieces, then spread on paper and allow to dry thoroughly. Store in a covered container.

Rice

Rice that is treated so it will be quick-cooking has been treated with chemicals to reduce the cooking time. White rice of any sort has had many of the nutrients removed—brown rice is a whole and valuable food.

Cooking Brown Rice

Wash and drain the rice, then stir it in a saucepan over a high flame for 1 minute, dry. Add twice the amount of boiling water and cover, then reduce the flame to the lowest possible. Let the rice cook, covered, for 45 minutes—do not stir, stirring during cooking makes brown rice gummy. Remove rice from the heat and let it stand, covered, for several minutes, to steam and dry some more. Add salt just before serving, stirring it into the rice.

▲ Edible Weeds

Burdock

Peel and steam stems, roots, and young flower stalks; peel young stems and serve raw in salads.

Caraway

The young leaves, roots, and shoots can be used raw to flavor salads, and the roots can be steamed as a vegetable and the leaves added to soups.

Cattail

Young stems, peeled, can be used raw in salads; discard the first 12 inches above the root. The pioneers dried and ground the root and used it as meal; it can also be added to soups.

Chickweed

The raw leaves can be used in salads, or the leaves can be quickly steamed.

Chicory

Serve the basal leaves raw in salads or add them to soup. The second-growth leaves are sold as endive. Chicory root can be dried, roasted, and

▲**Caution:** *Many plants or parts of plants are poisonous. Be sure that you have correctly identified any plant before eating.*

ground and used with coffee or as a coffee substitute; as a coffee substitute, boil 1 rounded teaspoon per cup of water for 5 minutes.

CRESS

Not only watercress but also bitter cress and scurvy grass can be served raw in salads; they can be added to soups as well.

DANDELION

The greens can be served raw in a salad or steamed and served as a vegetable; the Chinese method is to stir-fry dandelion greens in a little hot oil for 3 to 5 minutes.

DAYFLOWER

The leaves can be steamed as a vegetable or added to soup.

EVENING PRIMROSE

The roots can be used in soups, as can the leaves.

FIREWEED OR GREAT WILLOW HERB

The young stems and leaves can be added to soups, and the young shoots steamed as you would asparagus.

JERUSALEM ARTICHOKE

The tubers on the root can be baked or boiled, as you would treat potatoes.

LAMB'S QUARTERS

Young ones can be served raw in salads; older ones can be steamed as a vegetable. This was a favorite among the Indians.

MALLOW (CHEESE, HIGH, WHORLED, AND CURLED)

The young shoots can be used raw in salads, the leaves and stems added to soups. Hollyhock, a family member, has leaves that can be steamed and eaten.

▲ Marsh Marigold or Cowslip

The leaves can be steamed and served buttered or with cream sauce.
▲ **Caution:** *Do not eat raw; they are unsafe in that state.*

Pigweed or Green Amaranth

The young leaves can be served raw in salad; less-young leaves can be added to soups.

▲ Purslane or Wild Portulaca

Leaves can be served raw in salads; they can also be steamed, along with the fleshy stems, and served as a vegetable or added to soups.
▲ **Caution:** *Choose purslane with care, as milk purslane, for instance, is poisonous.*

Sorrel (mountain, alpine, sheep)

Serve this raw in salads or add to soups.

Thistle

Russian and sow thistles: cook the very young tops. *Stinging thistles:* steam the tops when young or add them to soups. *Elk and Indian thistles:* steam the roots.

Part III.

In the House

DRAINS

Cleaning Drains

Smells and grease in drains can be attacked by pouring in hot salt water—1 cup salt to 4 cups hot water.

Clogged Drains

Dissolve 1 pound washing soda in 3 gallons boiling water and pour through drain.

FIREPLACES

Removing Stains on Brick Tiling of Fireplaces

Most of these stains can be removed with a stiff brush and some vinegar.

▲ Free Fireplace Logs

Roll up your old newspapers. Roll them tightly—and make each roll about 6 inches in diameter, then fasten it by fully spreading out 2 more sheets, placing the roll on the corner and rolling diagonally, tucking the ends of the 2 sheets into each end of the log roll. The paper logs burn slowly and admirably.

▲ **Caution:** *Check with the newspaper office to see that the ink on the newspapers does not contain lead.*

Coloring Fireplace Flames

Soak fireplace logs in water solutions of these chemicals and then dry them, *or* sprinkle the powdered chemicals on the flames.

Chemical	Color It Produces
Borax	Green

Calcium chloride	Orange
Copper chloride	Blue-green
Copper nitrate	Emerald green
Lithium chloride	Purple
Salt	Yellow

Increasing Flame in a Fireplace

A scant handful of salt sprinkled over the flame will increase the flame (more than a scant handful, though, and the salt becomes a fire extinguisher).

Fragrant Kindling

Dried lemon peels and orange peels are good kindling, and pleasantly fragrant.

Fire Starters

Dip short pieces of kindling wood—or compact wads of newspaper tied with string—in melted paraffin and allow to cool.

GLASS

Cleaning Bottles with Narrow Necks

Use hot water with a teaspoon of vinegar, plus a few dried beans or some rice. Shake well.

Cement for Glass

Canada balsam makes a good transparent cement for glass.

Removing Scratches on Glass

Cigarette ashes, slightly moistened with water, will remove small scratches on a watch crystal—rub them over the glass. If there are deeper scratches, rub with moistened pumice first, then with the cigarette ashes. Jeweler's rouge may also be used—if you have an electric fingernail buffer. Put jeweler's rouge on the nail buffer and buff the scratches. This works well for scratched windscreens.

Washing Windows and Mirrors

Add either a little vinegar or a little household ammonia to the hot water you use for washing the windows. After rinsing, again with hot water, dry the windows with crumpled newspaper to prevent streaking and to increase the shine.

HOUSEPLANTS

Air in Houseplant Soil

Use a fork to aerate the soil around your houseplants once a month. Put the tines in only about ½ inch, and work from the outside in.

Sterilizing Soil for Houseplants

Approximately 5 pounds of soil can be spread out in a shallow baking pan and baked for 30 minutes at 250° F. to sterilize the soil without killing useful nutrients.

Watering Houseplants

If your tapwater is heavily treated, freeze it and defrost it to room temperature before using it on plants; this will deactivate much of the ingredients harmful to plants. If you do use tapwater directly, and it is heavily treated, cover the soil around your houseplants with ⅛ inch purified charcoal.

Tap a terra-cotta pot that has a houseplant in it on the side with a table knife; if what you hear is a ringing sound, the soil is dry. A dull sound means the soil is moist.

▲ Wick Watering

Make ½-inch-wide strips of wick from an absorbent cotton fabric—from old socks or folded over and stitched dishtowels. Poke one end into the hole in the bottom of the plant pot, being sure it goes into the soil; put the other end into a jar or glass filled with water, and cover the water jar with plastic film secured by string or a rubber band. Be sure the string or rubber band goes under the protruding wick, not on top of it, cutting off the water supply. Covering the plant or the water jar, or both, with transparent plastic will increase the moisture the plant gets.

▲**Caution:** *Do not use wick watering on plants that need very dry soil; do not use covering plastic on plants that need a dry atmosphere.*

Leaving Houseplants on Their Own

Up to 2 Weeks

Fill the bathtub with 6 inches of water; invert terra-cotta pots in it; and set the plants, in their own pots, on top of the inverted pots. Cover the tub with transparent plastic, taping the plastic to the tub rim. Leave the bathroom light on.

Up to 7 days

Put bamboo sticks into the pots, water the plants thoroughly (water until the water comes through the bottom of the pot), drop a plastic bag over the top, and tape the plastic to the pot. Set it on pebbles in 1½ or 2 inches of water.

Pests on Houseplants

Mealybug

A furry-looking white patch that does not move can be a cluster of mealybugs. If you catch this infestation in the early stages, dip a Q-Tip in rubbing alcohol (or vodka) and rub it on the white mealybugs. The next day, spray off the alcohol with water. Another method is to mix rubbing alcohol (or vodka) and water in equal portions and use it as a spray.

In later stages, you'll have to spray the leaves with a malathion solution, or put malathion in the soil.

Isolate any plant with mealybugs. If the plant recovers, transplant it in fresh soil; mealybug eggs are laid in the soil.

▲ Red Spider or Mite

If the houseplant leaves turn silver or yellow, look for a bit of red dust on their undersides. Those are red spiders, or mites. You can see them move under a magnifying glass. Spray with a malathion solution or mite spray.

▲ Aphids

These are small, winged insects. Use a malathion spray.

▲ Scale

This occurs mostly on ferns. Use a malathion spray or a nicotine sulphate solution (Black Leaf 40).

▲**Caution:** *Malathion is toxic. Keep away from children and pets.*

MARBLE

Marble Cleaner

Wrap a cloth around the cut edge of half a lemon, wet it in warm water and dip it in borax; rub the marble.

Removing Stains from Marble

1 pound washing soda   5⅓ cups hot water

Mix the washing soda in the hot water and apply it with a paint brush.

▲ Removing Iron Mold or Ink Stains from White Marble

1½ ounces oxalic acid   3 cups distilled water
¾ ounce butter antimony   Flour

Dissolve the oxalic acid and butter antimony in the water, then add sufficient flour to make the mixture the consistency of paste. Apply the paste to the marble with a brush and let it remain a few days. Wash off with clean water.

▲**Caution:** *Do not spill oxalic acid on clothes or skin.*

Polishing Black Marble

½ ounce gum elemi
2 ounces methylated spirit
4 ounces linseed oil

5 ounces turpentine
½ ounce acetic acid
3½ ounces water

Dissolve the gum in the spirit, and strain; add the oil and turpentine, and finally the acid and water.

Ink for Use on Stone or Marble

Mix equal parts of Trinidad asphaltum and oil of turpentine. This is used in a melted state for filling in letters cut on stone or marble, and is very durable.

Cement for Marble

Soak plaster of paris in a saturated solution of alum, dry it, then bake in the oven. After baking, grind it to a powder. It is then used as wanted, being mixed with water like plaster and applied. It sets into a very hard composition, capable of taking a very high polish, and may be mixed with various coloring minerals.

PETS

Removing Chlorine from Aquarium Water

The cheapest and best way is to let tapwater stand in open containers for a day or two before adding it to the aquarium. You can hasten this by heating the water to about 110° F. (not higher, though); when the water has cooled to 75 or 80 degrees, it is ready for use.

or

Stir in a little sodium thiosulfate, or photographer's "hypo"; about ½ grain in 1 to 6 gallons of water, depending on the concentration of chlorine. Buy it at a photographic supply store, not a pet store—you can get a pound for the price of a grain.

FIREARMS

Cleaning Firearms

WHEN A GUN IS IN GOOD CONDITION

First use a soft rag soaked in coal oil, then a stiff brush soaked in the same oil, and finally a clean, dry, soft rag. Each operation should be performed about a dozen times before the next is proceeded with. (The use of wire brushes for cleaning guns is objectionable because the sharp points cut into the tube.)

IF THE BREECH MECHANISM IS STIFF

Soak it in coal oil, then take it to pieces; let the parts remain in a bath of coal oil overnight, then rub them with a cloth dipped in the oil and sprinkled with some finely powdered bath brick.

Black for Gunsights

1 teaspoon fine lampblack
⅓ ounce spirit varnish
½ ounce methylated alcohol

▲Bluing Stain for Gun Barrels

4½ ounces hyposulfite of soda
¼ ounce acetate of lead

Mix the hyposulfite of soda into 1 quart water; mix the acetate of lead in another quart of water. Combine the two solutions and bring to a boil in a nonmetal pot. Clean the gun barrel free of grease, oil, or varnish; warm it; and smear with the hot solution, using a piece of sponge tied to a stick. When the color develops, wash and wipe dry. Finish with boiled linseed oil. ▲**Caution:** *Acetate of lead is very toxic. Use with great care.*

FABRIC CARE

▲ Javelle Water

4 pounds bicarbonate of soda   1 pound chloride of lime

Put the soda into a kettle over a high flame. Add 1 gallon boiling water; let it boil 10 to 15 minutes; then stir in the chloride of lime, free from lumps. Use when cool.

or

½ pound chloride of lime   7 ounces carbonate of soda
6 cups water   crystals
2 cups water

Mix the chloride of lime in the 6 cups of water. Separately, mix the carbonate of soda crystals in the 2 cups of water. Then mix the two solutions, stir well, and after the mixture has settled, draw off the clear liquid.

Either of these formulas will make an effective chlorine bleach.

▲ **Caution:** *Do not allow any acid—such as lemon juice—to combine with Javelle Water or any other chlorine bleach: the combination forms a poisonous gas.*

Stain Removal

HEAVY STAINS

Use 2 tablespoons washing soda in 1 cup lukewarm water.

DIRTY DIAPERS

Presoak in baking soda and water.

FRUIT AND WINE STAINS

Apply corn starch immediately, then soak in milk before washing.

GREASE STAINS

Treat fresh grease spots with corn starch, then pour boiling water or baking soda on stains before washing.

Ink Stains

Blot up carefully and apply corn starch. Soak in milk.

Bloodstains

Soak in cold water.

▲ Iron Stains

Dip the rust-stained portion of the clothing first in cold water, then in a strong solution of oxalic acid, then in rapidly boiling water, holding it in the steam for a few minutes. (The steam seems to be necessary with the acid.) If the spot does not disappear quickly, repeat the process. Rinse thoroughly. ▲**Caution:** *Do not spill oxalic acid on clothes or skin.*

Mildew Stains on Colored Cotton

Soak the fabric 24 hours or more in sour milk or buttermilk, then rinse in water and wash in strong soapsuds.

Mildew Stains on White Cloth

Moisten the spots repeatedly with Javelle Water diluted with 2 parts water; rinse well, then wash in strong soapy water that is not too hot.

Mildew, Wine, and Fruit Stains on Silks or Linen

Cut ordinary good soap into shavings and boil into a stiff paste with pure water. Apply this to the stain, and scatter on it some finely powdered potash. Then spread the fabric in the sun and allow it to remain there for 24 hours. When dry, sprinkle some water on the stain, then wash the fabric.

Perspiration Stains

Soak the fabric 1 hour in salt water—¼ cup salt to 4 cups water.

Rust Stains on Cotton or Linen

Wet the rust-stained portion of cotton or linen with lemon juice, then set it out in the sun.

Setting Dye in Cotton

Soak the cotton 20 minutes in salt water—½ cup salt in 4 cups water.

Wool

▲ Acid Test for Wool

Mix 2 drops of sulfuric acid with 100 drops of water and put a drop or two of the mixture on the cloth to be tested, allowing it to penetrate completely. Then place the sample between two sheets of paper and press with a hot iron for 1 minute. If the material contains cotton, the spot where the acid was placed becomes charred. When you rub the charred spot gently between your thumb and forefinger, the cotton falls away and leaves behind it whatever wool the material contains.

▲**Caution:** *Do not spill sulfuric acid on clothes or skin. Can cause severe burns.*

Waterproofing Canvas, Duck, or Other Close-Woven Cotton

Dissolve soap powder (not detergent) in hot water and add a solution of iron sulphate. The combination will produce a blob on the bottom of the container (don't use an iron container) that is an insoluble iron soap. Discard the liquid; wash the iron soap repeatedly in clear water, then let it dry thoroughly. Mix in enough linseed oil to make a thin paste that spreads easily and apply it to the fabric. The fabric will repel water, yet still be flexible.

▲ Waterproofing Woolen Fabric

Dissolve 4 ounces powdered alum and 4½ ounces sugar of lead (acetate of lead) in 3 gallons water; stir twice a day for 2 days. When perfect subsidence has taken place, pour off and save the clear liquid only; and add to the liquid ⅓ ounce of isinglass previously dissolved in warm water, taking care to mix the two solutions thoroughly. Steep the fabric in this mixture for 6 hours; do not wring. Hang up to drip dry.

▲**Caution:** *Acetate of lead is very toxic. Use with great care.*

FURS

Softening Fur Skins

Mix bran and water, making a paste; to every 2½ gallons of this paste, add 3½ ounces of glycerin. Apply this mixture to the skin, and when dry, brush off again; pull and rub the skin until it becomes soft. An alternative preparation is the yolks of 3 eggs, 7 cups water, and 1 ounce epsom salts.

Cleaning Furs

Rub into the fur a mixture of cornmeal or sawdust dampened with dry-cleaning solvent, then shake the fur out and let it dry. *After* it is dry, brush the fur or comb it lightly; hang the fur outdoors to air, in the shade.

CLEANING DARK FURS

Heat a quantity of new bran in a pan, taking care that it does not burn; stir constantly. When well heated, rub it thoroughly into the fur. Repeat two or three times. Shake the fur and brush briskly until it is free from dust.

Dyeing Furs

Hair dyes can be used to dye faded furs. Dip the fur in the dye quickly, wash it right away, shake out the moisture. Let the fur dry before brushing or combing it lightly; hang it outdoors to air, in the shade.

Making a Bearskin Rug

Remove all fatty matter from the inside and soak in warm water for 1 hour; then mix ½ ounce each of borax, saltpeter, and sulfate of soda (for each bearskin) with sufficient water to make a weak paste. Spread this paste over the inside of the skin with a brush, applying more to the thicker parts than to the thinner. Fold the skin with the flesh part inside, and put in a cool place; let it stand 24 hours. Wash the skin clean, and apply in the same manner as before a mixture of 1 ounce sal soda, ½ ounce borax, and 2 ounces hard white soap, melted slowly together without being allowed to boil. Fold the skin again, flesh side inside, and put away in a dry place for 24 hours.

Next, dissolve 4 ounces alum, 8 ounces salt, and 2 ounces saleratus in sufficient hot water to saturate the skin. When mixture is cool enough not to scald the hands, place the skin in it and allow it to remain 12 hours; then wring out and hang up to dry. When dry, repeat the soaking in the alum mixture and the drying several times, to make the skin soft. Last, smooth the inside of the skin with fine sandpaper and pumice stone.

LEATHER

Saddle Soap

7½ ounces soap powder	2½ ounces neat's-foot oil
36 ounces water	4 ounces beeswax

Dissolve the soap in hot water. Heat the neat's-foot oil and wax together until the wax is melted, then pour into the hot soap solution. Stir until thickening begins and pour into containers.

Removing Stains from Tan Shoes

Apply white castile soap with a piece of moistened absorbent cloth.

Cleaning Buckskin

Rub plenty of soft soap into the leather, and allow it to soak in a weak solution of washing soda in warm water for 2 hours. Then rub the leather sufficiently, and rinse in a weak solution of warm water, soda, and yellow soap. It must not be washed in pure water or it will become very hard when dry; it is the small quantity of soap remaining in the leather that makes it soft and pliable. After rinsing, wring out in a towel and dry quickly; then pull it in every direction, and brush well.

Indian Tan for Buckskin

The following is the Indian method of tanning buckskins for moccasins: Take a skin, either green or well soaked, and flesh it with a dull knife. Spread it on a smooth log and grain it by scraping with a sharp instrument; then rub nearly dry over the oval end of a board held upright. Take the brains of a deer or calf, dry by the fire gently, put them in a cloth and boil until soft; cool off the liquid until blood-warm, with water sufficient to soak the skin in, and soak until quite soft and pliable; then wring out as dry as possible. Wash in strong soapsuds and rub dry and smoke well with wood smoke. Instead of brains, oil of lard may be used and the skin soaked therein 6 hours.

U.S. Government Harness Dressing

1 gallon neat's-foot oil
2 pounds bayberry tallow
2 pounds beeswax
2 pounds beef tallow
2 quarts castor oil
1 ounce lampblack

Put into a pan over a moderate fire the neat's-foot oil, bayberry tallow, beeswax, and beef tallow. When the mixture is thoroughly melted, add the castor oil and lampblack. Stir well and strain through a cloth to remove any sediment. Allow to cool.

Farm and Team Harness Dressing

3 pounds beef tallow   1 pound neat's-foot oil

Heat the beef tallow—this should not be heated sufficiently to cause it to boil—then pour in gradually the neat's-foot oil and stir continually until the mixture is cold. A small quantity of lampblack may also be added for color.

SOAP

Old Soap for New

Chop or shave the leftover ends of bars of facial soap and place in a jar with a little boiling water. The result is a soap jelly, good for washing anything that can be washed with soap, and especially good for hand-washing fine fabrics. Add some sal soda and use to wash painted woodwork.

Rinsing Out Soap

A soapy feeling can be eliminated by adding vinegar to rinse water.

WALLPAPER

Wallpaper Paste

2 pounds fine flour	1 teaspoon finely powdered alum

Put the flour in a pail and add cold water gradually until it forms a thick paste, stirring well. Add the alum, then pour in gradually, constantly stirring, 6 quarts boiling water. Use when it has cooled.

Cleaning Wallpaper

Very stale bread rubbed over the wallpaper—in one direction only—does the job.

▲WHITEWASH

½ bushel lime
8 quarts salt
2½ pounds rice

½ pound powdered Spanish whiting
1 pound clean glue

Slake the lime with boiling water, covering to keep in the steam. Strain the liquid through a fine sieve and add the salt, which has previously been dissolved in warm water; add the rice, which has previously been boiled to a thin paste and kept boiling hot; add the whiting and the glue, which has been previously dissolved by soaking it well. Put the whole mixture in a small kettle within a large kettle filled with water, and hang over a slow fire. Add 5 gallons of hot water to the mixture, stir it well, and let it stand for a few days, covered. Coloring matter, with the exception of green, may be added. The whitewash should be put on quite hot.

▲**Caution:** *Lime is caustic and should be kept away from clothes and skin.*

WOOD

Oak

To Darken Oak

The wood to be darkened should be in a dark and airtight room. Pour a cup or so of liquid ammonia into a soup plate and place the plate on the floor in the center of the room. Seal any cracks around doors or windows with tape.

The ammonia does not touch the oak, but the gas that comes from the ammonia acts on the tannic acid in the wood and browns it so deep that a shaving or two may actually be taken off without removing the color. The depth of shade will depend entirely on the quantity of ammonia and the length of time of exposure.

Oak-colored Stain for Wood Floors

Dissolve permanganate of potash in water, dilute with more water, and apply a little, with a brush, to a piece of smooth board the same material as the floor. When it is first applied it produces a wine color, but after exposure to the air it becomes a rich oak shade. Expose your sample board to air for 30 minutes; if the color is too dark, the stain can be further diluted with water until the desired shade is produced. Use on a floor that is very clean and dry.

Polishes and Waxes

Furniture polish

1 quart boiled linseed oil	2 cups turpentine

Mix the oil and the turpentine, and store in a covered jar.

Instant Furniture Polish

Use any light medicinal or mineral lubricating oil. Apply with a soft cloth and polish with another clean one.

Wax for Old Furniture

Melt 1 pound of pure beeswax in a vessel placed in hot water—but not over an open flame. Add 1 pint of gum turpentine, remove from the hot water, and stir constantly while the mixture cools. Package in a wide-necked container before it really hardens.

Apply with a soft cloth. Let stand until solvent evaporates, then polish with a clean cloth.

Wax vs. Polish for Wood Floors and Furniture

Wax requires buffing; polish does not, or at least it doesn't require so much. Wax lasts a great deal longer, though, and it protects the wood more effectively. In most cases, the same wax or polish used on wood floors is suitable for wood furniture.

Once a year or so, the undersides of wooden tables and chairs should be waxed, as well as the tops; otherwise the wood will be sealed on only one side, and there is a chance that it will warp.

Stain Removal

REMOVING WHITE STAINS AND RINGS FROM WOOD

Place a thick towel or a thick blotter over the white stain, and apply a warm iron; the stain evaporates into the towel.

Repairs on Wood

REPAIRING "BLISTERS" IN FURNITURE VENEER AND REATTACHING VENEER THAT HAS SEPARATED

Cover with some heavy paper and press down for a minute with a hot iron. When you take the iron off, slide on a book or a block of wood and place something heavy on top of it until the veneer has cooled.

If the blister is large, cut it so it can be flattened before the heating procedure.

REPAIRING GOUGES AND BURNS IN WOOD FURNITURE

Put masking tape around the scar; heat a spatula on the stove and press it against a shellac stick, letting the melting shellac drip onto the scar. When sufficient shellac has dripped in, level off the mound with the spatula. When it is completely hardened, rub the mound down level with a piece of fine sandpaper that is dampened with alcohol, and go over it afterward with 000 steel wool. Then polish or wax.

REPAIRING SUPERFICIAL SCRATCHES IN WOOD FURNITURE

On dark woods, use crayon or shoe polish, rub off excess with a soft cloth, then polish or wax.

On dark mahogany, use iodine.

On light wood, apply mayonnaise, leave it on for 24 hours, then rub it into the wood and wipe off the wood.

Filling Cracks in Wood

Cracks in furniture and other woodwork can be filled with wood sawdust mixed with thin liquid glue. Let it harden slightly, then rub the spot with fine sandpaper.

METAL

Cleaning Metal Files

▲ Iron or Steel Particles

Immerse the files for several minutes in 1 ounce sulfuric acid and 4 ounces water (add the acid to the water, not the water to the acid), then brush with a stiff wire brush. Next, wash the files in plain water, then coat them slightly with machine oil or penetrating oil diluted slightly with gasoline. Wipe off the excess.

Lead and Brass Filings

These can be removed with a stiff brush.

▲ Aluminum Filings

Soak the files in a warm lye solution. Wash the files well and oil as before.

There is a special short-bristled wire brush called a "file card" available at hardware stores that may eliminate the need for chemical cleaning in some cases.

Polishing Chrome

Rub the chrome with dry baking soda on a dry cloth.

Preventing Nickel from Tarnishing

To prevent nickel-plated articles from tarnishing when not in use, smear them over with a mixture of 4 parts Vaseline, 1 part paraffin wax, and 1

▲**Caution:** *With either sulfuric acid or lye, use a glass dish, wear rubber gloves, and do not spill on clothes or skin. Take particular care to keep them away from the eyes.*

part finely powdered quicklime. Wrap them with paper smeared on one side with the mixture.

▲ Removing Rust from Iron or Steel

Attach a piece of ordinary zinc to the articles to be treated and let them lie in water to which a little sulfuric acid has been added. Keep them immersed for several days or a week, until the rust has entirely disappeared. If there is much rust, a little more sulfuric acid should be added occasionally. The essential part of the process is that the zinc must be in good electrical contact with the iron; a good way is to twist an iron wire tightly around the object and connect this with the zinc. The iron is not attacked in the least as long as the zinc is in good electrical contact with it. Afterward, the treated articles should be washed and oiled.

▲ Removing Rust from Nickel Plate

Cover the stains with oil or grease for a few days, then remove the rust by rubbing with a little ammonia. If this does not remove the rust, try very diluted hydrochloric acid; wash off with water, and when dry, polish with whiting.

Brass and Copper Polish

Mix equal parts of flour and salt and add vinegar to make a stiff paste; spread the paste thickly on the brass or copper and let it dry. Then rinse and wipe off the paste.

Cleaning Burned Pots

Either scrub the burned pot with cleansing powder and a copper scouring pad (steel-wool soap pads are a waste of money and leave rust stains on the sink and sometimes bits of steel wool that are hard to see and rinse out in the pot); *or* put the pot on the burner with a few inches of water and a teaspoon or more of washing soda in it and boil; with a really bad burn, do both. If you are out of washing soda, putting some cleansing powder and household bleach in with the boiling water will sometimes do. Vinegar boiled in the pot will also work on burned aluminum pots.

▲**Caution:** *Sulfuric acid and hydrochloric acid are extremely caustic and can cause severe burns. Do not spill on clothes or skin.*

Removing Cabbage or Fish Smells from Pots

Put vinegar into the pan and boil it for a minute or two.

Polishing Silver

In 1 quart water in a large aluminum pot, put 1 tablespoon each salt and baking soda. Bring to a boil; add 4 or 5 pieces of silverware (not including silverware that's held together with glue) and let them boil 3 minutes or so; then remove and add the next 4 or 5 pieces.

Storing Silverware

Wrap individual pieces in aluminum foil if you have no tarnish-proof chest.

LIGHTER FLUID

Use V.M.&P. naphtha—a high-grade benzine; buy it in a hardware store and save money. It will be easy to insert in the lighter if you use an eyedropper.

OVENS

Oven Cleaning

Just before bedtime, turn on the oven for a few minutes to heat it, then turn oven off and set a small dish of household ammonia inside it. In the morning, remove the ammonia and wipe the inside of the oven with a damp cloth—all or most of the charred grease will have loosened. If there is still charred grease, repeat the operation the next night.

Temporary Brick Oven

Unglazed terra-cotta floor tiles, ½ to 1 inch thick

Before the first use, soak the tiles 24 hours in water, and let dry 2 to 3 hours. Cover the middle shelf rack of your oven with one layer of the tiles;

preheat for 30 minutes. After the first use, no further soaking will be necessary.

Brick ovens traditionally make the finest pizza.

PORCELAIN
Cleaning Porcelain

Baking soda on a damp cloth is an effective cleaner for oven doors, refrigerator doors, and the like.

REFRIGERATORS AND FREEZERS
Deodorizing Refrigerators and Freezers

Either put a small amount of uncompressed charcoal in the refrigerator (or freezer), replacing it with new charcoal once a day until the odor has gone, or wash the insides with 4 tablespoons baking soda dissolved in 2 quarts hot water.

Preparing Freezer for Defrosting

After the freezer or the freezing part of the refrigerator has been defrosted, spray it with alcohol, line it with heavy-duty aluminum foil, or coat it with unsalted solid shortening (such as Crisco) or unsalted margarine. Defrosting will not have to take place again as soon as it would have without this treatment; and when it must be done, it will be less work.

PIANOS
Whitening Ivory Piano Keys

Make a paste from whiting and solution of potash; lay it on the keys and allow it to remain about 24 hours.

BOOKS

Removing Grease Spots from Books

OLD GREASE SPOTS

Mix caustic potash and hot water for a 3 to 5 percent solution, according to the age of the stain. Saturate a piece of thick blotting paper with the solution and apply it to the other side of the page; place two or three leaves of dry blotting paper on one side of the page; press on the dry blotting paper with a hot iron. If the first application does not remove the stain, repeat the operation. When the grease is removed, dip another sheet of blotting paper in a 4 to 5 percent solution of hydrochloric acid and water, apply it to one side and fresh dry blotting paper to the other side of the page, and iron until the page is dry. This will restore the faded printing.

FRESH GREASE SPOTS

Blotting paper saturated with benzine, chloroform, or rectified oil of turpentine will answer.

WAX STAINS

The treatment is the same as that used for grease spots, except that as much wax as possible should be scraped off the surface first.

▲Repairing Torn Book Pages

Japanese tissue or lens tissue

Book paste:
⅓ ounce corn starch
7 ounces water
1 teaspoon precipitated chalk (calcium carbonate)
Few drops of formalin

Make a paste of the starch and the precipitated chalk; allow it to stand at least 15 minutes, with frequent stirring, to allow the starch to swell. Pour, slowly and with continuous stirring, into 6 ounces vigorously boiling water. The starch should be thoroughly wetted, and the water kept at a vigorous boil to ensure success. Heat in a double boiler—with continuous stirring—about 1 hour; then cool and add a few drops of formalin as a preservative. Add more or less water as necessary, as there is quite a bit of variation among starches from different packagers. **Note:** *Alum should never be used as a constituent of starch paste.*

Apply the paste to the paper, not to the tissue. Place tissue (with paste on it) on the torn area, smooth it, and cover it with wax paper. Put under pressure for smooth drying.

Use tissue on both sides of any repair that is larger than 1 inch square, and to mend any strip tear with tissue that is wider than ¾ inch, or the paper will curl.

▲**Caution:** *Formalin can irritate the skin.*

CANDLES
Preventing Drips in Candles

2 ounces epsom salt
13 ounces water
2 ounces dextrin

Dip the candles in the solution, then let them dry.

ANIMAL HORNS
Mounting Horns

Fill the animal horns with wet plaster of paris and insert in each horn a piece of wood longer than the hollow. When the plaster is dry, the wood will be solidly set in, and the protruding wood can be fastened where the horns are wanted.

Polishing Horns

First scrape the animal horns with glass to take off any roughness, then rub well with a piece of cloth wetted and dipped in powdered pumice, until a smooth surface is obtained. Next, polish with rottenstone and linseed oil, and finish with dry flour and a clean cloth. The more rubbing with rottenstone and oil, the better the polish.

Part IV.

Controlling Household Pests

▲ Ants

Locate the ants' nest, if possible. It may be outdoors, or it may be in the house—within a wall or partition, under flooring, or under a pile of papers. You may be able to trace the ants from the food source to the approximate location of the nest.

If you find the nest, treat it with a liquid household insecticide containing diazinon, lindane, malathion, or propoxur.

Apply the insecticide as a surface spray. For kitchen treatments, apply the liquid with a small paintbrush to surfaces over which the ants are crawling in their line of march. Treat all cracks, openings, or runways they may be using to enter the house or to enter a room.

Allow a few days for the ants to reach the insecticide deposits. If the pests continue to appear, they probably are entering over surfaces you have not treated. ▲ **Caution:** *Lindane and malathion are toxic. Keep away from children and pets.*

▲ Bats

Sometimes bats enter a home and establish their roost in the attic, in a space between the walls, or in an unused part of an upper story.

Normally bats are harmless, but they are subject to rabies and can transmit it to humans. A bad odor emanates from their droppings and urine and persists long after a roost is broken up; this may attract a new colony of bats.

Cover openings through which bats might enter with sheet metal or ¼-inch-mesh hardware cloth.

It may be necessary to fumigate the infested areas. ▲ **Caution:** *This operation is dangerous. Do not attempt it yourself. Employ a professional exterminator.' Never handle live bats; you may be exposed to rabies. Wear rubber gloves when picking up and destroying dead bats.*

▲ Bedbugs

Evidences of bedbug infestation (other than itching bites) are black or brown spots on surfaces where the bugs have been resting; these spots are digested blood. There usually is an offensive odor in rooms where bedbugs are numerous.

Once bedbugs enter a house, only the application of insecticide will remove them. Household surface sprays containing lindane, malathion, ronnel, or pyrethrum are usually effective against bedbugs. Sometimes the bugs are resistant to lindane. Lindane, ronnel, or malathion may require only one application; pyrethrum usually must be applied several times at intervals of 1 or 2 weeks.

Spray the slats, springs, and frames of beds. Apply enough spray to wet them thoroughly. Cover the mattresses completely with spray, but do not soak them; be sure to get the spray into seams and tufts.

▲**Caution:** *Do not treat mattresses with a spray containing more than 0.1 percent of lindane or 1 percent of malathion; higher concentrations of these materials are not safe to use on mattresses. Allow mattress to dry before use.*

Spray baseboards and the openings or cracks in walls and between floorboards. If some bedbugs are present several weeks after treatment, spray again.

▲Centipedes

To kill these basically harmless pests, use a household surface spray containing lindane. Apply the spray directly on the pests. Sweep them up.

▲**Caution:** *Lindane and malathion are toxic. Keep away from children and pets.*

Clothes Moths and Carpet Beetles

The larvae of clothes moths and carpet beetles attack clothing and a wide range of household furnishings including blankets, rugs, carpets, drapes, pillows, hair mattresses, brushes, and upholstery.

To control them you must clean your home often enough to prevent lint, dust, and hair from accumulating.

One way to protect fabrics, clothing, blankets, and other susceptible materials is to spray them with a stainless household insecticide containing methoxychlor, Perthane, or Strobane. The insecticide should be packaged and labeled for this purpose. Spray lightly and uniformly with insecticide until surfaces are moist. Do not soak or saturate. If the articles are soiled, have them dry cleaned before treating.

Treat surfaces over which insects are likely to crawl with a spray that contains 3 to 5 percent of premium-grade malathion or ronnel, or ½ percent of lindane or diazinon. Use a coarse spray. Do not use aerosols for surface spraying.

See that closets or containers used for storage are made as airtight as is practicable. A closet should be tightly closed, and the cracks around the door sealed with tape or rope putty. Place paradichlorobenzene crystals, or naphthalene flakes or balls, in the closets or containers before sealing them. In a trunk-size container, use 1 pound of crystals, flakes, or balls; in a closet, use 1 pound for each 100 cubic feet of space. The vapors are heavier than air. Therefore the chemicals should be placed in a shallow container on a shelf, or suspended from a clothes rod or hook in a thin cloth bag or perforated container. *Keep out of reach of children.*

Woolens can be protected from feeding damage by wrapping them in paper or sealing them in a cardboard box into which some of the crystals, flakes, or balls have been placed.

It is recommended that furs be protected from insect damage during the summer months by placing them in commercial storage where they will receive professional care and can be insured against damage.

Cockroaches

See *Roaches.*

▲ Crickets

Close all openings to the house. Tighten screens, windows, and doors. If the crickets still persist in entering, use a household spray containing lindane, or malathion. Apply it around baseboards, in closets, and in cracks where the crickets may hide. Dusts containing these insecticides may be used on bare concrete floors of basements or out-of-the-way locations elsewhere in the house.

▲ Fleas

Thoroughly clean infested rooms with a vacuum cleaner; include carpets, rugs, upholstered furniture, and other items on which eggs or larvae may be. Then apply a surface spray containing methoxychlor, malathion, pyrethrum, or ronnel. Be sure to use a nonstaining product when spraying

▲**Caution:** *Lindane and malathion are toxic. Keep away from children and pets.*

rugs, carpets, and upholstered furniture. Treat baseboards, cracks in the floor, rugs, carpets, furniture, and places in the home where the pet habitually sleeps. You may need to repeat the treatment after about a week.

The best way to prevent flea infestations in the house is to control fleas on the pets. A dust containing 4 or 5 percent of malathion or 5 percent of methoxychlor is safe and effective when applied directly on dogs or cats. Rub it into the fur, to the skin.

House Flies

House flies breed in places where garbage or manure accumulates. Clean up these places. See that your garbage cans are equipped with tight-fitting lids; dispose of garbage at least once a week—more often in summer. Promptly dispose of the droppings of pets. Do not allow food to stand where it will attract flies.

Keep house flies out by placing screens in your windows and doors. See that screened doors swing outward. Screens that have 14 meshes to the inch will keep out house flies; if the screens have 16 meshes, they will also keep out many smaller insects. In a humid climate, use screens of copper, aluminum, bronze, plastic, or one of the rust-resisting alloys.

If you need an insecticide to control the flies in your home, apply a household space or aerosol spray. Be sure the container label says the spray is for *flying insects;* follow the directions.

Fly Paper

Coat stiff paper with one of the following mixes:

1 pint resin	¼ ounce linseed oil

Dissolve by the aid of gentle heat, and while warm, spread on the paper.

or

9 parts resin	4 parts rapeseed oil

Heat until thick enough, and spread on the paper.

or

8 parts resin	4 parts turpentine
4 parts rapeseed oil	½ part honey

Heat until thick enough, and spread on the paper.

or

1 pound resin
3½ ounces molasses

2½ ounces linseed oil

Boil until thick enough, and spread on the paper.

▲ Mice

Seal any holes in the walls, floors, and foundation of the house, and see that food is not left in places where mice can get to it.

If there are only a few mice in your home, they can usually be disposed of with ordinary snap traps. The traps should be placed along walls and near holes. Place them at a right angle to the walls so the trigger mechanism will intercept the mouse's probable route of travel.

One of the best baits to use in snap traps is peanut butter smeared over the trigger surface. Other good baits are cake, flour, bacon, nutmeats, cheese, and soft candies, particularly milk chocolate or gumdrops.

With large infestations, where mice are so numerous that trapping is impractical, poison bait may be used. Purchase materials labeled for this purpose.

▲ **Caution:** *Follow the directions and observe all precautions on the container label.*

Avoid placing the materials where there is danger of contaminating food supplies. Pesticides should never be left within reach of children, irresponsible persons, pets, or livestock.

▲ Mites

The kinds of mites that may bite humans are rodent mites, bird mites, certain food mites, and chiggers. These pests seldom transmit human diseases, but their bites cause swelling, severe itching, and sometimes fever. A chigger attached in a pore of the skin or at the base of a hair may become so enveloped in swollen flesh that it appears to be burrowing into the skin.

Clover mites sometimes infest homes and may become a nuisance, but they do not bite people.

Rodent or bird mites can infest and breed in a home where rats or mice or pet birds are present. Bird mites can also enter the home from wild birds that are nesting in a chimney or near a ventilator opening; or they may be carried in from a pigeon or poultry coop on your premises.

Food mites breed in certain foods, such as cheese and grains, and may cause skin rash when they get on humans.

Chiggers breed on the ground—not in the house. They may be brought into the house on clothing or pets and may cause trouble for a short time, but they cannot breed indoors.

To prevent mites from biting you, apply a repellent to your person and clothing. Use a repellent containing deet, ethyl hexanediol, dimethyl carbate, or dimethyl phthalate; these are available at drug, hardware, or sporting goods stores. Itching caused by mite bites may be relieved by applying an ointment containing benzocaine.

You can rid your home of mites that attack people by treating infested places with a household surface spray containing malathion.

If you are troubled by rodent mites, first apply a spray to kill them; then rid your home of the rats or mice from which the mites come.

To eliminate the sources of bird mites, get rid of nests near openings in the house. Clean up bird coops and treat them with a surface spray containing malathion.

If food mites are a problem, first get rid of the infested foods. Prevent infestations by keeping all foods well covered, and by keeping shelves free of spilled food. Infested shelves may be treated with a household surface spray containing not more than 2 percent of malathion. *Do not contaminate food or utensils with the insecticide.*

▲**Caution:** *Malathion is toxic. Keep away from children and pets.*

Mosquitoes

EXAMINING FOR SIGNS OF PRE-ADULT MOSQUITOES

Examine any standing water once a week for the presence of mosquito larvae. Use a white pan or cup to dip out water, since the larvae are more easily seen against a white background. Eggs are elongate, about $\frac{1}{40}$-inch long in most species, and dark brown or black when ready to hatch. They are laid in batches of 50 and more. Larvae (wigglers) are tiny and wormlike; they change to pupae in a week, comma-shaped forms that are sometimes called "tumblers" because of their tumbling motion when disturbed in the water. Pupae transform into adults in about 2 days.

▲ Killing Pre-Adult Mosquitoes

On water that will not be used for drinking by humans, animals, or fish, and that will not be used as a birdbath, use:

3½ teaspoons of 55 percent malathion emulsifiable concentrate   Water in kerosene or fuel oil

Mix the malathion with enough of the other liquid to make 1 pint spray. Apply 1 ounce of spray to each 100 square feet of water surface. Do not use fuel oil or kerosene on vegetation.

or

2¼ teaspoons of 20 percent lindane emulsifiable concentrate   Water, kerosene, or fuel oil

Mix the lindane with enough of the other liquid to make 1 pint spray. Apply 1 ounce of spray to each 100 square feet of water surface.

or

On water that will not be used for drinking, or for a birdbath, *and that does not contain emergent vegetation,* apply full-strength fuel oil or kerosene at the rate of 2 to 4 ounces to each 100 square feet.

▲ Residual Sprays for Killing Adult Mosquitoes

1½ fluid ounces of 20 percent lindane emulsifiable concentrate   Water, kerosene, or fuel oil

Mix the lindane with enough of the other liquid to make 1 quart of spray. Apply in a coarse spray to the foundations and underparts of buildings, around buildings, between logs, and on tree trunks. Apply to the point where runoff occurs. Do not use on vegetation.

or

1¼ ounces of 25 percent lindane wettable powder   Water

Mix the lindane with enough water to make 1 quart of spray. Apply in a coarse spray to the foundations and underparts of buildings, around buildings, between logs, on tree trunks, and to the undersurfaces of leaves. Apply to the point where runoff occurs. May be used on vegetation, but avoid flowering plants—bees may be killed.

▲ **Caution:** *Lindane and malathion are toxic. Keep away from children and pets.*

▲ Space Sprays for Killing Adult Mosquitoes

¾ fluid ounce of 20 percent lindane emulsifiable concentrate   Water, kerosene, or fuel oil

Mix the lindane with enough of the other liquid to make 1 quart of spray.

or

1¾ fluid ounces of 55 percent malathion emulsifiable concentrate   Kerosene or fuel oil

Mix the malathion with enough kerosene or fuel oil to make 1 quart.

or

1½ fluid ounces of 55 percent malathion emulsifiable concentrate   Water, kerosene or fuel oil

Mix the malathion with enough of the other liquid to make 1 quart.

▲ Fogs for Killing Adult Mosquitoes

1¾ fluid ounces of 55 percent malathion emulsifiable concentrate   Kerosene or fuel oil

Mix the malathion with enough kerosene or fuel oil to make 1 quart of spray.

Either ¾ fluid ounce of 20 percent lindane emulsifiable concentrate *or* 1½ fluid ounces of 55 percent malathion emulsifiable concentrate   Kerosene or fuel oil

Mix *either* the lindane *or* the malathion with enough of the other liquid to make 1 quart of spray.

▲ **Caution:** *Lindane and malathion are toxic. Keep away from children and pets.*

Repelling Mosquitoes and Other Insects

Vitamin B^1 taken orally can repel insects, according to several studies. A study in Mexico was reported as finding that the following amounts—200 milligrams for adults, and 100 milligrams for children—were most effective, diminishing the number of insect bites and the itching.

Repellents Used on Skin

Against mosquitoes, biting flies, gnats, and chiggers, use:
Full-strength ethyl hexanediol
Dimethyl phthalate

Apply to skin; keep away from eyes. Of these chemicals, deet is the most effective against most kinds of insects. All these chemicals may damage painted surfaces; dimethyl phthalate damages plastics. On the skin, these repellents will be effective for 2 or more hours, if not washed off before that time. On clothing they will be effective for several days if the clothing is not washed or wetted during that time. These repellents will not damage nylon, polyester, acrylic, all-cotton, or all-wool cloth; they may cause temporary stains, however.

▲ Pantry Pests

Keep pantry shelves clean. If you are troubled by a persistent infestation of pantry pests, treat your kitchen cupboards with insecticide. Apply a household surface spray containing not more than 2 percent of malathion.

Spray lightly, only when the shelves are empty. When the spray dries, cover the shelves with clean paper or foil before placing packages of food in the cupboard.

Inspect food packages. Do not put infested products on your pantry shelves.

Sterilize doubtful products in the oven at about 140° F. for 30 minutes or in a home freezer held at 0° F or below for 3 or 4 days.

Store uninfested or heat-sterilized dry foods in clean metal or glass containers that have tight-fitting lids, such as coffee cans or fruit jars. See that the covers fit tightly enough to prevent tiny insects from crawling in.

▲**Caution:** *Malathion is toxic. Keep away from children and pets.*

▲ Rats

Leave no food in open places; this includes food in unopened cardboard containers. Place garbage and refuse promptly in tightly covered metal containers.

Keep storage places orderly and clean. Stack lumber, boxes, cartons, and other objects on racks at least 1 foot above the floor.

If your house has double walls with spaces between ceilings and the floors below, make sure the spaces are tightly sealed.

Poisoned bait is recommended as the best means of killing rats. Purchase a suitable bait, labeled for this purpose. Follow directions on the label and observe the precautions to the letter.

▲**Caution:** *Poisons should never be left within the reach of children, irresponsible persons, pets, or livestock.*

Traps are recommended where infestations are very small, or as a follow-up after the use of bait.

Close all holes in exterior walls. See that spaces around doors, windows, and other necessary openings are no larger than ¼ inch. If rats are a serious problem in your neighborhood, install self-closing devices on frequently used doors to the outside.

▲ Roaches

Boric acid should be sprinkled generously in all the corners and dark spots roaches lurk in, and left there. Put new powder down every 6 weeks or so. It doesn't smell and it isn't sprayed into the air you breathe—and it kills the roaches that walk through it, though it takes a couple of days to have effect. Flypaper on flat surfaces such as shelves or walls will trap roaches, too.

▲**Caution:** *Do not put boric acid where children or pets might get at it.*

▲Scorpions

The best way to keep scorpions out of the home, or to kill them if they already are in, is to use a household surface spray containing lindane. Apply the spray to baseboards, around window and door casings, and to the foundation of the house.

On the outside, use the spray also to treat the lower parts of tree trunks, stumps, piles of lumber, and rock walls. A waterbase spray is preferred for outdoor use; ready-to-use household sprays often contain oils that may burn vegetation.

▲**Caution:** *If scorpions are in your neighborhood, do not have a children's sandbox in which the pests may lurk.*

If a scorpion should sting you, call your physician at once; the first 6 hours after a sting are the most critical.

▲**Caution:** *Lindane is toxic. Keep away from children and pets.*

▲ Silverfish and Firebrats

Apply insecticide in the form of a surface spray or a dust. The results may not be immediate; but if the insecticide is properly and thoroughly applied, it will leave a residue that should be effective within a few weeks. If satisfactory control is not achieved in 2 or 3 weeks, make additional applications.

If you are troubled with firebrats but not with silverfish, you may need to apply insecticide only to warm parts of the house.

In applying sprays, use a household spray containing lindane, diazinon, ronnel, malathion or propoxur. Apply the spray to baseboards, door and window casings, closets, and places where pipes go through walls. Some sprays have oil-solution bases; do not apply these near electric motors, gas pilot flames, or other places where they may start fires.

In applying dusts, use a dust containing not more than 6 percent of chlordane, 1 percent of lindane, or 5 percent of malathion. Apply the dust with a hand duster. Blow it into cracks and on surfaces of the places recommended for sprays. Dusts may be applied safely to places where oil-solution sprays might start fires.

▲ Spiders

Remove loose brick, wood, tile, or trash from around the yard or basement where the spiders may live or hide. Use a stick or broom to knock down webs, spiders, and egg sacs. Crush them underfoot. Apply a pesticide to spider-infested areas. Use a household spray containing lindane.

Many spiders are not only non-poisonous but helpful to humankind in that they catch and eat flies, and even mosquitoes.

▲**Caution:** *Do not spray spiders overhead. A spider hit by the spray may drop straight down but still be capable of biting for some time. Beware of black widow spiders. Call a doctor immediately if bitten.*

▲**Caution:** *Lindane and malathion are toxic. Keep out of reach of children and pets.*

Termites

The techniques of termite control are too extensive for adequate discussion here. A pest-control operator has the experience and equipment to solve the problem.

▲ Ticks

Treatment should start with the dog.

Buy an emulsifiable concentrate containing 50 percent of malathion. Mix 1 tablespoon of the concentrate with each gallon of water. Dip the dog in the mixture. Do not include his head, but sponge his ears with the mixture if necessary. For a large dog, make up the mixture in a bucket and pour it slowly over the dog's back; make sure it soaks through the hair to the skin.

To get rid of new broods of ticks that are developing in the home, use a household insecticide containing lindane, malathion or diazinon. Spray or paint it on cracks in the floor, around baseboards and window casings, on places where the dog habitually sleeps, and on other places where ticks may be hiding. Repeat after 2 or 3 months. A malathion spray may be applied to rugs, carpets, or upholstered furniture. Be sure the container label states that it will not stain.

▲ **Caution:** *Lindane and malathion are toxic. Keep out of reach of children and pets.*

▲ Wasps

Treat the nest with a household surface spray or a dust containing chlordane. Direct the insecticide as closely as possible into the nest opening.

For outside use, a water-base spray is preferable to one having an oil base. Apply it with a household or garden-type applicator.

If you use a dust, apply it with a hand duster or garden-type duster. The extension tube of a garden-type duster may be inserted into the nest opening; two or three strong puffs of dust will filter through the nest, and usually will kill the colony within 24 hours.

After treating an underground nest, throw a shovelful of moist earth over the entrance. This will prevent the dying wasps from reaching the surface.

All treatments should be made at night, when there is less danger of being stung. ▲**Caution:** *If a person with a history of asthma, hayfever, or other allergy is stung by a wasp, his or her physician should be notified immediately.*

▲ Pesticide for Killing Wood-Destroying Beetles

2 percent chlordane *or* 0.5 percent lindane in deodorized kerosene (such as deobase or ultrasene)

In crawl spaces, use a powersprayer and a coarse spray. Indoors, use after removing finish from the wood; if removal is impractical, treat the wood but do not touch it until it has been dry for several hours. When treating above a finished ceiling, avoid using too much material, since it may seep through and cause stains. Also use sparingly on parquet floors, to avoid dissolving the asphalt bonding cement. On furniture, after removal of finish if practicable, the pesticide can be put into individual holes with a small brush or a plastic squeeze bottle equipped with a tube. Do not treat parts of furniture that people will touch.

▲**Caution:** *A fine mist may explode if ignited. In any use of this pesticide provide plenty of ventilation and keep away from flame or lighted cigarette. Keep away from children and pets.*

Part V.

In the Garden

PLANTS THAT HELP AND NEED HELP

Ant Repellent

To keep ants from your home, plant mint and tansy by doorways.

Apple Tree Pests

Spray in early spring, before the buds appear, with miscible oil and water.

APPLE MAGGOT FLY

In each of several jars, mix 1 part blackstrap molasses, 9 parts water, and 1 yeast cake. Let the mixtures sit for 48 hours, then hang the jars in the tree to catch the apple maggot fly.

CODLING MOTHS

Mix 2 gallons water with 1 ounce ryania.

APPLE BORERS

Use boiling water.

Asparagus

Parsley, tomatoes, and rue should be planted over the asparagus bed as pest repellents. If Japanese beetle grubs get in, plant white geraniums. Spread chickfeed and bread crumbs to keep the house sparrows visiting—sparrows eat the asparagus beetle. Plant nasturtium, asters, and zinnia to repel cucumber beetles.

Basil Leaves

Crushed and diluted, these are used in Israel as an insecticide. Basil plants, grown next to tomatoes, repel most tomato-attracted insects.

Beans

Plant beans in the same spot where cabbage, Brussels sprouts, or broccoli were the year before. Beans should be planted with some garlic in between, every 4 or 5 feet. Or use onions, scallions, leeks, and shallots to substitute for some of the garlic, although garlic is the best insect repellent.

BEAN ANTHRACNOSE AND BACTERIAL BEAN BLIGHT

Spray the bean plants with 1 part garlic juice in 20 parts water.

APHIDS ON BEANS

Put shiny strips of aluminum foil on the ground beside the rows, and plant nasturtiums in the rows. If aphids come, hose the bean plants (especially the undersides of leaves), then spray with garlic and water in a 1-to-20 ratio.

BEAN FUNGI

A preventive, in or on the soil, would be oat straw, mature soybean hay, or corn stover. If a fungus appears, mix wood ashes with lime and apply.

BEAN RUST

Dust the bean plants with garlic powder, or spray them with water and garlic, in a 20-to-1 ratio.

Beets

To combat the flea beetle, thin young beets, and use onion spray on them—one medium onion, pulverized in the blender, mixed with 3 cups of water.

Cabbage

Cabbage should not be grown in the same spot two years running. It should follow beans, corn, lettuce, onions, or peas. Sow hyssop next to cabbages to help keep white butterflies and club root off cabbage. Plant peppermint nearby to repel aphids.

Cabbages with "Club Root"

This is caused by nematodes, so grow marigolds near your cabbages, and grow marigolds where you plan to plant cabbages next year. Plow the marigolds under when they have finished flowering.

Cabbage Cutworms

Fit a tarpaper collar around each cabbage stem.

Cabbage White Maggots

Lay a circle of tarpaper on the soil around each stem, to prevent maggots from laying their eggs there.

Cabbage Worms or Cabbage Butterflies

Lay out wood ashes between the rows of plants when the white butterflies come.

Carrots

Carrots should not be grown in the same spot two years in a row; they should be grown where cabbage, broccoli, or Brussels sprouts have been the year before.

Carrots Stored in the Ground

Cover the row with several inches of autumn leaves, which will prevent the carrot roots from freezing. Chantenay carrots stored this way will be crisp and sweet when dug out during the winter.

Carrots Attacked by Carrot Fly

When this happens, grow a few sage plants in the row with carrots.

Catnip

This is a good pest repellent.

Celery

Do not plant celery where lettuce or cabbage has been planted within a few years.

Celery Attacked by Nematodes

This will show browning in the rootlets and/or whitening in the leaves. Plant marigolds nearby, and plant marigolds where you plan to plant celery for next year. Plow under the marigolds when they have finished flowering.

Chicory in the Cellar

At the end of autumn, cut the tops off the chicory in the garden within 1 inch of the crown. Lift out the roots gently and plant them in damp sand or soil in the cellar or a dark closet; keep out all light.

Chives

Chives planted under roses control black spot on the roses. Chives grown next to carrots add to the carrots' growth and flavor.

Corn

Do not plant corn and tomatoes near each other—corn is attacked by the same pests that attack tomatoes, the corn earworm or tomato fruitworm. If you get the worms, apply ¼ teaspoon mineral oil to the silk end of the ear when the silk starts to turn brown; this is where the eggs are laid. Black-light traps can be used to catch the moths before they lay their eggs; these traps will also catch the moths that lay eggs in May that will become European corn borers. They are also useful against striped cucumber beetles.

Cucumbers

Cucumbers, dwarf beans, and squashes should be planted near to sweet corn. Cucumber beetles, which infest both cucumbers and squash, may be driven away by radishes planted among the affected plants. Plant calendulas and marigolds there, too. The striped cucumber beetle may be defeated by sufficient moisture; if it does appear, use a dusting of wood ashes, rock phosphate, or granite dust, or a wood-ash spray (wood ashes and hydrated lime in water). Planting the cucumbers near onions or garlic is helpful; so are nearby beans, corn, and peas, and the weeds lamb's quarters and sow thistle.

Currants

Do not grow currants or gooseberries where there are nearby white pines—a pest that is attracted to the berries causes blister rust on white pine.

Dill

Dill plants trap tomato worms.

Elderberry

Elderberry leaves can be used to make lilac and purple dyes.

Garlic

Plant garlic around your peach, apple, and pear trees, and your roses. Garlic, onions, scallions, leeks, and shallots can be planted around the edge of the garden to repel rabbits and woodchucks. To keep Japanese beetles away from asparagus, plant grapes and white roses; then spray the beetles off the grapes and roses with a garlic spray.

Japanese Beetles

Plant white geraniums near corn or other plants that are bothered by Japanese beetles; the white geranium acts as a repellent.

To kill Japanese beetles: Every 3 feet put 1 teaspoon of *Bacillus popillae* into the ground; it kills these beetles' larvae, but nothing else.

Jewelweed

Jewelweed (wild touch-me-not or *Impatiens capensis*), or the liquid from it, is praised as a preventive for poison ivy rash. Indians used to use the juice on itchy skin. It can be used as a fresh liquid, or the liquid can be frozen.

Kale

Pests on kale may include flea beetles, aphids, and female Herculean beetles. Mint, thyme, catnip, hyssop, and rosemary are good repellents to plant nearby.

Marigolds

Mexican marigolds, *Tagetes minuta,* are most valued among the marigolds as pest deterrents.

Mice and Mole Repellents

Plant wormwood *(Artemisia absinthium)* with camomile and spurge.

Milkweed

This can be used as a trap plant for leafhoppers.

Mint

This is a repellent for aphids.

Nasturtiums

Nasturtiums will help to keep aphids away from cabbage, cauliflower, broccoli, and Brussels sprouts; and in a greenhouse they repel whitefly. Yellow nasturtiums are effective repellents of aphids. They do best in poor soil.

Nematode Repellents

Plant marigolds, both where you have plants that might be attacked by nematodes and where you'll have such plants next year. When they have finished blooming, plow them under. When beans and cucumbers are planted together with marigolds, the beans provide good shade for the cucumbers, and the cucumbers and marigolds repel pests.

Onions

Onions should not be grown near peas or beans. Onions grown in a row can be attacked by the onion maggot; if onions are grown all around and through the garden (except near peas and beans), the maggot has less chance, and the onions also protect the other plants by repelling a large variety of pests. Around the border of the garden, onions repel rabbits and woodchucks.

Parsley

This is a protective plant next to hybrid tea roses.

Parsnips

Parsnips stored in the ground all winter should be dug up at the onset of warm weather.

Peas

Plant peas one year after growing broccoli, Brussels sprouts, or cabbage in the spot, and plant carrots, onions, parsnips, or lettuce between the peas. Plant a little mint in the row with the peas.

Potatoes

For potato bugs and/or potato beetles—spray with basil, and mulch deeply, or sprinkle bran.

Rabbit Repellent

Onions. Also see page 117.

Radishes

Radishes, planted near corn and cabbage, attract maggots away from the corn and cabbage.

Squashes

See "Cucumbers"—the same pests are attracted, and the same repellents work.

Rhubarb

Do not allow dock near your rhubarb plants—it will attract the curculio, a pest to rhubarb, into the neighborhood. Dig up rhubarb roots in autumn, store them in sand outdoors until after the first hard frost, then put them in soil in the cellar to grow winter rhubarb.

Rosemary

This is a pest repellent.

Tansy

This is a pest repellent, especially a repellent of flying insects.

Thyme

Thyme grown next to cabbages, cauliflower, broccoli, or Brussels sprouts repels cabbage rootflies. Thyme is also a general pest repellent.

Tomatoes

Tomatoes are repellents to the asparagus beetle. Do not grow tomatoes, potatoes, and eggplants near each other; similar diseases and pests attack them all. Do not grow tomatoes near corn. Plant dill among tomatoes to help keep the tomatoes pest-free.

Turnips

Turnips are repellents of aphids, beetles, house flies, and spider mites. On young turnips attacked by flea beetles, use a dust of wood ashes.

Weevil Repellent

Mix wormwood *(Artemisia absinthium)* and water in a 1-to-10 ratio in the blender for a spray.

Woodchuck Repellent

Onions.

Sweet Woodruff

This is a moth repellent for inside the closet.

Yarrow

This is a pest repellent.

Zinnia

Zinnias are trap plants for Japanese beetles.

GENERAL CARE

General Insect Repellent

Mix wormwood *(Artemisia absinthium)* and water in a 1-to-10 ratio, with ½ clove garlic, in the blender for a spray.

Nettle Spray

Put stinging nettle leaves in a blender with water, with or without garlic, marigold, or mint, for a garden spray.

Winter-Made Spray

1 medium onion	1 teaspoon very hot red pepper
3 cloves garlic	

Grind these in the blender with some water; add enough more water to make a quart. Strain the mixture through a nylon stocking into your sprayer, or into a container for freezing.

Insect Traps

CONE TRAP

Construct a wooden frame for a box 2 feet high, 1 foot long, and 1 foot wide. Attach small-mesh screening to the sides and bottom. Set a shallow pan in it with sweetened water, or an attractive smelling oil, to lure insects. Attach a cone of wire to the top of the box, wide at the top and narrowing until it ends an inch or so above the liquid in the pan. Insects that may be trapped this way include moths of many varieties, cabbage loopers, wire worms, cucumber beetles, and corn borers.

HOPPING-INSECT TRAP

Fill a trough with water topped with kerosene; extend one of the long sides of the trough up 3 feet as a backboard, to knock the pests back when they jump up to escape. The backboard might also be coated with a sticky substance such as tanglefoot.

HANGING TRAP

Coat pieces of cardboard or scraps from discarded tires with tanglefoot and suspend them from tree limbs or poles.

EARWIG TRAP

Cut 1-foot lengths of bamboo or discarded garden hose; place them among the plants for several days and nights, and earwigs will crawl into them. Carry two flat pieces of wood or tile with you to clap onto either end of the piece of hose and lift it; dump out the earwigs into a can of water with a top layer of kerosene, or dump them into a pond for the frogs to eat.

Rabbit Deterrent

Mix coal tar, nicotine, alcohol, and turpentine—60, 30, 5, 5—together. Impregnate a rope with the mixture and run the rope around the garden 4 inches above the ground.

Mice and Mole Foil

To keep these pests away from bulbs, for each bulb purchase a 1-foot length of wire cloth (½-inch mesh) and make a circle of it, fastening the cut ends together. The cage does not need to be more than 8 inches long. Bury the cage around the bulb when you plant it—with the top an inch or so below the surface of the soil.

To repel mice from gardens generally, plant wormwood with camomile and spurge.

Changing the Soil Quality

To make it more alkaline, add lime.
To add nitrogen, add bloodmeal.
To add magnesium, add an epsom-salt solution.
To make a soil more acid, add pine needles, sawdust, peat moss, or tanbark.

LAWNS

Fungus Diseases That Affect Lawns

Helminthosporium Leafspot and Foot Rot

One of the most widely distributed and destructive grass diseases. Damage is most conspicuous in the leaves—reddish-brown to purplish-black spots appear on leaves and stems; leaves shrivel and the stems, crowns, rhizomes, and roots discolor and rot. Dead grass in attacked areas often is attributed to drought injury. The disease occurs mainly during cool, moist weather, but it may develop during summer, too. Pure stands of Kentucky bluegrass are ideal for development of this disease—mixtures of several species of grass retard its development.

Mow the grass to 1¾ to 2 inches rather than ½ to 1 inch; apply enough fertilizer to keep grass healthy; avoid overstimulation with nitrogen, particularly in the spring. Remove clippings.

Fading Out

This disease is caused by a complex of Helminthosporium and Curvularia species, and is most destructive during hot, humid weather. Diseased areas appear yellowed or dappled green—when the disease becomes severe, the grass "fades out," leaving dead grass in irregular reddish-brown patches 2 to 3 inches across.

The same management practices and fungicides recommended for controlling Helminthosporium leafspot are recommended for this.

Brown Patch

Brown patch occurs during warm, wet weather, and is most damaging following excessive applications of nitrogen. In irregular circular areas—inches or feet in diameter—a brownish discoloration appears. In bentgrasses, a narrow, dark, smoke-color ring borders the diseased area. The fungus threads, or mycelium, are frequently seen as filmy white tufts early in the morning while the dew is on the grass.

Avoid excessive applications of nitrogen; water early in the day to give grass leaves time to dry before night; remove clippings.

Rust

Rust fungi, which attack many lawn grasses, usually come in late summer and remain until frost. Yellow-orange or red-brown powdery pustules develop on leaves and stems—if a cloth is rubbed across the affected leaves, the spores adhere to the cloth and produce a yellowish or orange stain. Merion Kentucky bluegrass is especially susceptible—damage is less severe if that grass is mixed with common Kentucky bluegrass or with red fescue. Recommended mixtures are 50-50 Merion and common red fescue; or 50-25-25 Merion, common Kentucky bluegrass, and red fescue.

Pythium Diseases

The two most destructive diseases Pythium causes are grease spot and cottony blight. The fungi are destructive at 70° F. and above, especially in humid areas and in poorly drained soils. Injury is most noticeable in early morning as a circular spot or group of spots about 2 inches in diameter surrounded by blackened blades intertwined with the fungus threads. Diseased leaves become water soaked, mat together, and appear slimy; they soon wither and become reddish brown. Grass is usually killed in 24 hours and it lies flat instead of remaining upright like grass killed by the brown patch disease. New grass does not grow back.

Avoid watering methods that keep foliage and ground wet for long periods. Avoid excessive watering in warm weather; and delay seeding until fall.

Dollar Spot

Also known as small brown patch. It is most destructive during cool, wet weather—it generally attacks in May and June, stops for two months, and starts again in September and October. Bleached spots the size of a silver dollar appear, and the turf is left pitted.

Damage usually is greatest if there is a deficiency of nitrogen.

Stripe Smut

Narrow gray or black stripes—which may be continuous or discontinuous—develop lengthwise in leaf blades, then the diseased leaves wither, curl, and shred, from the tip downward, and die. Diseased plants are shorter than neighboring healthy plants, and may be obscured by them.

Smut damage is less severe if Merion Kentucky bluegrass is mixed with common Kentucky bluegrass, or if smut-tolerant varieties like Gylking, Park, or Pennstar are grown.

Snow Mold and Fusarium Patch

Snow mold symptoms appear first as a white cottony growth on the leaves; as the leaves die, they turn light brown and cling together. Diseased areas are discolored dirty white, gray, or slightly pink. Fusarium patch causes irregular pale yellow areas—later, they become whitish gray, sometimes with a faint pinkish edge.

Do not apply high nitrogen fertilizers late in the fall—they might stimulate growth of the grass and result in active growth when snow covers the ground, which would favor the development of these fungi. Keep the lawn cut in the fall. Apply lime if soil tests indicate the need.

Mushrooms and Fairy Rings

Mushrooms that grow individually or in clumps usually are growing from buried wood. They are harmless to lawns, but they may be unsightly.

Eliminate mushrooms that grow from buried wood by digging up the pieces. If this is impractical, drench the soil with captan by punching holes 6 to 8 inches apart and 6 to 8 inches deep in the ground within and surrounding the infected area, then pour a solution of captan down the holes.

Fairy rings are circles, or arcs of dark-green grass surrounding areas of light-colored or dead grass. In spring and fall mushrooms develop in a circle outlining the fairy ring—which increases in size each year, unless the fungus is controlled. Fairy rings seldom occur in lawns that are adequately fertilized and treated with fungicides for control of other diseases. Fumigate the affected area or, alternatively, punch holes around the outside of the ring and throughout the affected area, then pour a solution of captan into the holes.

Slime Molds

Slime molds often cover grass with a dusty, bluish-gray, black, or yellow mass. Slime molds occur during wet weather; they disappear rapidly as soon as it becomes dry. The large masses can be readily broken up by sweeping with a broom, or by spraying with a strong stream of water. During prolonged damp weather, slime molds can be especially annoying, and it may be desirable to apply a turf fungicide.

Other Causes of Poor Turf

Undesirable Species

Short-lived perennials like redtop and ryegrass or weedy annuals such as annual bluegrass and crabgrass do not make a desirable lawn. Annual species usually die at the end of the growing season, and leave brown or bare areas that may be mistaken for disease injury.

GUIDE FOR SELECTING FUNGICIDES
Application Per 1,000 Square Feet — Follow Directions on Label

Disease and Causal Organism	Fungicide	Directions
Leafspot (Blight, Going-out, Melting-out) *Helminthosporium*	Acti-dione-thiram Captan Daconil 2787 Dyrene Fore Zineb	Disease can appear from April to August, depending on kind of grass and species of fungus. Treat your lawn every 7 to 14 days three times consecutively or until the disease has been controlled.
Brown Patch *Rhizoctonia solani*	Dyrene Fore PCNB	Disease can appear from June to August. Treat your lawn every 5 to 10 days until the disease has been controlled.
Rust *Puccina*	Acti-dione-thiram Daconil 2787 Zineb	Disease can appear from June to September. Treat your lawn every 7 to 14 days until rust disappears.
Grease Spot and Cottony Blight *Pythium*	Dexon Zineb	Disease can appear from July to September and in fall and winter during warm, humid periods in the South. Treat your lawn every 5 to 14 days until the disease has been controlled.

Disease and Causal Organism	Fungicide	Directions
Dollar Spot *Sclerotinia homeocarpa*	Acti-dione-thiram Daconil 2787 Dyrene Fore	Disease can appear from June to October. Treat your lawn at 7 to 14 day intervals until the disease has been controlled.
Stripe Smut *Ustilago striiformis*	Tersan 1991	Apply in October or early spring before grass begins growing. Water lawn well.
Snow Mold *Typhula*	Dyrene	Disease can appear from fall to spring. Treat your lawn at intervals of 2 to 6 weeks as needed.
Fusarium Patch *Fusarium*	Tersan 1991	
Mushrooms Fairy Rings *Marasmius, Psalliota campestris, Lepiota*	Captan Methyl Bromide	Disease can appear throughout the growing season. Pour double or triple strength concentrate of captan into 1-inch holes punched 4 to 6 inches deep and 6 to 8 inches apart both inside and outside the affected area. Alternative method: fumigate infected area with methyl bromide; reseed or resod.
Slime Molds *Physarum cinereum*	Fore Zineb	Disease can appear throughout the growing season and can be controlled without fungicides.

CAUTION: Do not graze treated areas or feed clippings to livestock or poultry.

Undesirable Mixtures

Bermudagrasses and zoysiagrasses turn straw colored or brown following a killing frost. When these species are grown in a sod composed mainly of cool-season grasses, a mottled brown and green lawn often results because of the differences in sensitivity to cold. This effect may resemble disease injury.

Insect Injury

Lawn grasses are often damaged by insect pests. For information concerning lawn insects and their control, see your county agent or write to the U.S. Department of Agriculture, Washington, D.C. 20250.

Fertilizer Burn

Concentrated inorganic fertilizers, if applied too heavily, burn grass in 2 or 3 days. Burned areas may occur in spots or streaks or the entire lawn may be damaged. To prevent injury, apply the fertilizer evenly in recommended amounts when the grass is dry, then water immediately. If burning occurs, water generously to wash off excess fertilizer and reduce injury.

Hydrated Lime Burn

Hydrated lime burns grass if it is applied unevenly and in large amounts. Ground agricultural limestone is safer and is usually recommended for lawns.

Pesticide Injury

Some of the chemicals used for disease, insect, and weed control are potent and may injure grass if improperly applied. Chemical formulations vary with manufacturers. Follow directions and observe all precautions on the label.

Dog Urine Injury

This kind of injury is frequently mistaken for disease damage. Affected spots are usually round or slightly irregular and variable in size. The grass within the spot turns brown or straw colored and usually dies.

Improper Mowing

Cutting grass too closely or too frequently may result in a condition that looks like disease. Cut Kentucky bluegrass, red fescue, and other grasses with upright growth habit to a height of 1¾ to 2 inches. Do not lower the height of cutting in midseason; it may result in serious injury. Mow the grass before it gets too tall; not more than one-half of the leaf surface should be removed at one time. The frequency of mowing will depend on quantity of fertilizer and water applied, weather conditions, and other factors that influence plant growth. Clippings need not be removed unless growth is excessive.

Improper Watering

Frequent light watering induces shallow rooting in grasses. Shallow-rooted grasses are readily injured during periods of severe drought. Frequent evening watering favors disease development because it keeps grass leaves moist for long periods.

Do not water grass until it begins to wilt, then apply enough water to soak the soil to a depth of 6 inches or more. It is more economical to water the lawn only when water is needed and it is better for the grass.

Buried Debris

A thin layer of soil over rocks or debris such as lumber, stumps, plaster, and cement dries rapidly and may not retain enough moisture to keep grass green. Correct this condition by removing the cause.

Accumulation of Runners

Another type of dry spot results when an accumulation of runners (thatch) in bermudagrass, bentgrass, and zoysiagrass becomes impervious and does not let water into the soil. Mowing following vigorous hand raking corrects this condition.

Compacted Soils

Saturated soils pack easily and bake hard when dry, especially where traffic is heavy. The soil may become packed so hard that water will not penetrate the surface. Grass then thins out and bare spots result. To correct this condition, loosen or perforate the soil with a tined fork or aerifying implement and, if necessary, fertilize and reseed the lawn.

BIRDS

Attach a string to the top of a pine cone. Force peanut butter into the lower $2/3$ of the pine cone with a butter knife, then roll it in birdseed. Hang the cone outdoors.

Familiar Birds and Their Preferred Plants

BALTIMORE ORIOLE—apple, cherry, elderberry, mountain ash, various berries.

BLUEBIRD—dogwood; also autumn olive, cherry, elderberry, holly, honeysuckle, mountain ash, pokeberry, red cedar, sumac, various berries.

BLUEJAY—oak; also cherry, elderberry, sunflower, wild plum, cultivated grains.

BUNTING, PAINTED AND INDIGO—elderberry, millet, sunflower.

CARDINAL—sunflower; also autumn olive, cherry, corn, dogwood, elderberry, millet, pokeberry, wheat, and seeds of grasses, weeds, and conifers.

CATBIRD—cherry and oak; also autumn olive, beautyberry, crabapple, dogwood, elderberry, firethorn, hawthorn, holly, honeysuckle, plum, pokeberry, sumac.

CEDAR WAXWING—cherry, crabapple, and hawthorn; also autumn olive, dogwood, elderberry, firethorn, holly, honeysuckle, pokeberry.

CHICKADEE—oak and sunflower; also autumn olive, crabapple, elderberry, millet, sumac.

DOVE, MOURNING AND GROUND—holly, millet, pokeberry, sunflower.

FINCH, PURPLE—cherry and sunflower; also autumn olive, crabapple, dogwood, firethorn, honeysuckle, millet, sumac.

GOLDFINCH—sunflower; also honeysuckle, millet, mulberry, oak, seeds of garden flowers, weeds, and conifers.

GROSBEAK, EVENING—cherry, dogwood, and sunflower; also crabapple, elderberry, honeysuckle, millet, oak, sumac.

JUNCO—millet and sunflower; also autumn olive, dogwood, elderberry, firethorn, holly, honeysuckle, oak, pokeberry, sumac.

MOCKINGBIRD—pokeberry; also autumn olive, beautyberry, cherry, crabapple, dogwood, elderberry, firethorn, hawthorn, highbush cranberry, holly, honeysuckle, oak, plum, sumac.

NUTHATCH—oak and sunflower; also autumn olive, crabapple, elderberry, millet, sumac.

ORIOLE—apple, cherry, crabapple, dogwood, elderberry, mountain ash, plum, pokeberry, sumac, various berries.

ROBIN—cherry, dogwood, holly, and sumac; also autumn olive, beautyberry, cotoneaster, crabapple, elderberry, firethorn, hawthorn, honeysuckle, plum, pokeberry, Russian olive, sumac, various berries.

SISKIN—sunflower; also honeysuckle, millet, oak.

SPARROW—millet and sunflower; also autumn olive, dogwood, elderberry, firethorn, holly, honeysuckle, oak, pokeberry.

TANAGER—cherry, crabapple, dogwood, elderberry, plum, pokeberry, sumac.

THRASHER, BROWN—cherry and oak; also autumn olive, beautyberry, crabapple, dogwood, elderberry, firethorn, hawthorn, holly, honeysuckle, plum, pokeberry, sumac.

THRUSH—dogwood; also autumn olive, beautyberry, cherry, elderberry, firethorn, holly, honeysuckle, pokeberry, sumac.

TITMOUSE—oak and sunflower; also autumn olive, crabapple, millet, sumac.

TOWHEE, RUFOUS-SIDED—sunflower; also cherry, crabapple, elderberry, holly, millet, oak, plum.

WOODPECKER—oak; also cherry, crabapple, dogwood, elderberry, firethorn, hawthorn, holly, honeysuckle, millet, plum, pokeberry, sumac, sunflower.

DOG AND CAT REPELLENTS

▲Repellent Powder

Shake in a bag to mix; sprinkle where desired.

1 ounce cayenne pepper
2½ ounces flour
1½ ounces powdered mustard

▲**Caution:** *Do not inhale the dust or get it in your eyes.*

▲Repellent Spray

To keep dogs and cats from outdoor wood, concrete, or stone, spray these with a concentrated solution of mothflakes (naphthalene or paradichlorobenzene) in mineral spirits or painter's naphtha. For a long time the residue will give off vapors repellent to both animals and moths.

▲**Caution:** *Do not prepare or use near fire or open flame.*

AUTOMOBILE CARE

Cleaner and Polish for Automobile

22 parts light mineral oil
1 part gum acacia, powdered
145 parts water
26 parts kieselguhr
6 parts glycerin

Put the gum acacia in a bowl and add a considerable part of the water all at once; then stir well until combined. Add the rest of the water and the other ingredients, stir well, or put in bottles. Shake well before each use.

▲Automobile Wax

2 parts carnauba wax
3 parts turpentine
2 parts ceresin
3 parts mineral spirits or V.M.&P. naphtha

Melt the waxes in a vessel placed in hot water—not over an open fire. Add the turpentine and mineral spirits or naphtha rapidly in a thin stream, constantly stirring. Cool the mixture rapidly, while stirring vigorously.

▲**Caution:** *Do not prepare or use near fire or open flame.*

Car Cooling System Cleaner

1 pound washing soda 3½ quarts warm water

Drain the cooling system, add the cleaner, and fill the system with water. Then run the engine at fast idling speed for about 20 to 30 minutes. Cover the radiator, if necessary, to build up and maintain a temperature of between 180° and 200° F.

At the end of this period, stop the engine and drain out the cleaning solution along with the dissolved and loosened scale, grease, and dirt. Then thoroughly flush the system with clean water.

Windshield and Window Defogger

Carry a cut raw potato along when you are driving in weather cold enough that water vapor condenses on your windshield and car windows. Rubbing the cut side on the inside surface of the glass will prevent this fogging. Lacking a potato and its juices, saliva will do the same, or even natural oil from the surfaces next to and around the nose.

Part VI.

Energy, Safety, and Miscellaneous Formulas

ENERGY

Electricity Used by Common Household Appliances

Appliance	Watts
Air conditioner, room	800 to 1500
Blanket	150 to 200
Blender	250
Clock	2 to 3
Coffeemaker	600 to 1000
Deep fryer	1200 to 1650
Dishwasher	600 to 1000
Dryer, clothes	4000 to 8700
Fan, portable	50 to 200
Food mixer	120 to 250
Freezer, home	300 to 500
Frying pan	1000 to 1200
Furnace blower	800
Garbage disposal unit	200 to 400
Grill	1000 to 1200
Heat lamp	250
Heater, portable home	600 to 1650
Heater, portable, home, 280-volt	2800 to 5600
Heating pad	50 to 75
Hot plate, each burner	550 to 1200
Iron, hand	660 to 1200
Ironer	1200 to 1650
Lamps, incandescent	2 up
Lamps, fluorescent	15 to 60
Motors: ¼-horsepower	300 to 400
½-horsepower	450 to 600
1-horsepower	950 to 1000
Projector, movie or slide	150 to 550
Radio, transistor	6 to 12

Radio, tube	35 to 150
Range, oven and all burners	8000 to 16000
Refrigerator	150 to 300
Roaster	1200 to 1650
Rotisserie-broiler	1200 to 1650
Sewing machine	60 to 90
Shaver	8 to 12
Stereo hi-fi	100 to 400
Television	200 to 400
Toaster	550 to 1200
Vacuum cleaner	200 to 800
Waffle iron	600 to 1100
Washing machine	400 to 800
Water heater	2000 to 5000
Water pump	300 to 700

A one-door refrigerator with manual defrost, 12 cubic feet, will generally use 2 kilowatts a day. A 14-cubic-foot frost-free two-door refrigerator-freezer will use 4 kilowatts a day.

In freezers, there is quite a difference in electricity use between chest-style and uprights. If each is 16 cubic feet, manual defrost, the chest will use less than 4 and the upright will use 5 kilowatts per day. A frost-free upright of the same size will use nearly 7 kilowatts in a day.

Gas Used in Household Appliances

	Approximate BTU Input per Hour
Oven or broiler	25,000
Each range-top burner	10,000
Refrigerator	3,000
Clothes dryer	35,000
Incinerator	32,000
Water heater (quick recovery), automatic storage:	
30-gallon tank	30,000
40-gallon tank	38,000
50-gallon tank	50,000

Water heater, automatic instantaneous:
2 gallon per minute	142,000
4 gallon per minute	285,000
6 gallon per minute	428,400

Natural gas, as piped into a household, has 400 BTUs (British Thermal Units) per cubic foot in many regions of the country; in such regions, divide the figures above by 400 to find the number of cubic feet of gas you must pay for when you use appliances.

In many households, by the way, the pilot light accounts for ⅔ of all the gas used in a month.

To Discover a Short in the Internal House Wiring

If a plug-type fuse has blown, and the short circuit does not seem to be in any of the appliances that were plugged in, it might be in the internal house wiring. To determine whether this is so, you must unplug every appliance and lamp on the circuit and remove all bulbs from wall or ceiling sockets on the circuit. Do not turn off any switches. Then substitute a 10- or 25-watt light bulb for the fuse in the fuse box—if the bulb lights, there is a short in the internal house wiring. Remove the bulb immediately. Do not replace the fuse—and call a licensed electrician to correct the wiring.

Finding Electricity

A few farmers in the Midwest who have electricity-carrying lines passing over their land have placed under the line a large magnet with heavy wire coiled around it, from which they are able to derive electric current. It is not yet clear whether the electric-power companies can legally stop this practice; so far, reports say, the farmers have won each case that has come to court. (However, this electricity does not produce satisfactory performance from, and may damage, many modern appliances.)

Electric Wire Size Guide (Copper Wire)

Minimum Wire Size, American Wire Gauge (AWG)

Current in amperes	10	13	15	18	20	25	30	40	55	70	80	95
Portable Cords: 2 conductor & ground	18	16	14	14	12	12	10	8	6	4	2	2
Permanent wiring: Indoor	14	14	14	12	12	10	10	8	6	4	3	2
Permanent wiring: Outdoor-single conduit in air	14	14	14	14	12	10	10	8	6	6	4	

Data are for commonly used rubber- or plastic-insulated cords and plastic-insulated wire (type TW) in 86° F. surrounding air temperature. The temperature around the wire is not always the temperature in the rest of the house, though—a wire on a water heater, or near a heat-producing motor, or light fixture, is in a hotter spot. For higher air temperatures, reduce current by the following percentages: 104° F., -18 percent; 113° F., -29 percent; 122° F., -42 percent; 131° F., -59 percent. For insulations allowing higher temperatures and currents, consult National Electric Code tables.

Suggested maximum lengths in feet of cords of wiring to connect 120-volt appliances or motors (based on 3 percent voltage drop in cord or wire). For 230-volt loads, double all lengths.

Wire Size AWG	\multicolumn{11}{c}{Current in amperes}

Wire Size AWG	5	10	15	20	25	30	35	40	45	50	55
6	875	437	252	219	175	146	125	109	97	88	80
8	550	275	184	137	110	92	79	69			
10	345	173	115	86	69	58					
12	218	109	76	55	44						
14	138	69	46								
16	88	44									
18	55	28									

At low currents, it may be possible to increase cord lengths. At high currents, satisfactory operation may require shorter lengths due to voltage loss in supply. If only incandescent lamps are connected, longer cord lengths will not cause damage, but lamp brilliance will be reduced.

If the appliance does not show what current in amperes it uses, divide the watt rating by the voltage rating.

Costs and Savings for Energy-Saving Home Improvements

	Cost	Savings
In the winter, turn thermostat down 6° F. from your usual setting	$0	$20-$65 each year
Put plastic storm windows on all your windows in cold weather (plastic storm windows are just about as effective as glass ones; they do, though, usually have to be replaced every year)	$5-$7 each year	$20-$55 each year
Have your oil furnace serviced	$25 each year	$25-$65 each year
Caulk and weatherstrip your doors and windows (do it yourself—it isn't hard, any hardware store has the materials, and having a contractor do it would cost twice as much)	$75-$105 (one-time cost)	$30-$75 each year
Insulate your attic (again, try to do it yourself—having a contractor do it would cost about twice as much)	$160-$290 (one-time cost)	$35-$120 each year

The figures above are supplied by the government and refer to the average house. The government also supplies easy-to-understand formulas for figuring out exactly what kind of energy-saving home improvements make sense for your particular house, what you need, how much it will cost, and how much it will save you in fuel bills. *In the Bank . . . Or Up* the Chimney? A Dollars and Cents Guide to Energy-Saving Home Improvements* is for sale from the Superintendent of Documents, U.S. Government Printing Office, Washington, D.C., 20402. The price is $1.70.

Fahrenheit and Celsius (or Centigrade)

On the Fahrenheit temperature scale, water freezes at 32° and boils at 212°; on the Celsius or Centigrade scale, water freezes at 0° and boils at 100°.

To convert degrees from Fahrenheit to Celsius, subtract 32 from the Fahrenheit number, then multiply the remainder by 5/9 (or 0.556).

To convert degrees from Celsius to Fahrenheit, multiply the Celsius number by 9/5 (or 1.8) and add 32.

▲ Battery Polarity Test

Immerse the bare ends of the leads from the battery ½ inch apart in a strong solution of salt water. ▲**Caution:** *If the battery is more than about 45 volts, place them farther apart and be sure the parts of the wires you hold are well insulated.* There will be more bubbles around the negative wire than around the positive.

Testing a Dry-Cell Battery (Flashlight Batteries, Etc.)

Stand the battery on a table. With one hand, hold the base of a flashlight bulb firmly against the battery's brass button. With the other hand, touch a pocketknife blade to the zinc at the outer edge of the battery top and at the same time to the metal part of the bulb. Make certain the blade is on the zinc, not the casing. If the bulb does not light—and if the bulb is good—the battery is dead.

A less-elegant but equally effective—and safe and easier—method is to lick the tip of your index finger, then touch your tongue to one of the battery's buttons and while your tongue's still there, put your damp index finger on the other button or on the battery's base. If there is an instant change in taste—a sudden metallic taste—the battery is alive. *Do not do this with a battery more powerful than 22½ volts.*

Tests for Acids and Alkalis

A water infusion of chokecherry will turn green when you add an alkali to it and light red when you add an acid. Crush the berries, pour boiling water over them, and let stand for 30 minutes, stirring occasionally. Strain out the berries and use the clear liquid.

Cooling with Chemicals

To cool a bottle of soda, fold a thick towel and wrap it around the sides and bottom of a large fruit-juice can for insulation. Then pour in 1 quart of the coldest water you can get, 1 pound of photographic hypo, stir rapidly, and insert the bottle of juice, soft drink, or whatever, that you want to cool. The temperature of the bottle should go down about 30° F. (The hypo solution need not be wasted. Bottle it and use it for preparing photographic fixing baths.)

A mixture of 50 parts ammonium chloride and 50 parts potassium nitrate, dissolved in 160 parts water, will produce even greater cold. A bottle originally at room temperature will drop to below 32° F.

Low-Melting-Point Alloys

There are a number of metal alloys that melt at the temperature of boiling water or even below this. Some of them are used to make trick spoons, which surprise those to whom they are furnished by melting in their tea or coffee. What is known as "D'Arcet's alloy" is composed of 8 parts bismuth, 5 parts lead, and 3 parts tin. This alloy melts below 212° F. Another alloy, which melts at 197° F., is made of 3 parts lead, 2 parts tin, and 5 parts bismuth.

FIRE RETARDATION

Fire Retardation in Fabrics

Glow retardants are more important in draperies, mattress covers, and the like; flame retardation is most important in personal clothing.

7 ounces borax	3 ounces boric acid
2 quarts hot water	

Make a paste of boric acid with a small quantity of water. Add this and the borax to water. Stir until the solution becomes clear; warm the solution if it becomes cloudy or jellylike.

Fabrics treated with this solution do not flame when exposed to fire. Glow lasts about 30 seconds. Re-treat within a year.

Do not use on rayon or resin-treated cotton that is crushproof, wrinkleproof, or wash-and-wear.

or

6 ounces borax
2 quarts water
6 ounces diammonium phosphate

Add chemicals to water. Stir until solution is clear. This formula is less flame retardant than the previous one, but is more glow retardant. It slightly reduces the strength of treated fabrics if not washed out within 3 or 4 months.

or

12 ounces diammonium phosphate   2 quarts water

Add chemical to water. Stir until solution is clear. Use this formula for resin-treated cotton or rayon fabrics. This formula is less flame retardant than the first formula, but has good glow-retardant properties. It has a greater tendency than the first two to weaken a treated fabric if the fabric is stored for long periods.

or

13 ounces ammonium sulfate   2 quarts water
Small amount of household ammonia

Add ammonium sulfate to water and stir until clear; then add enough ammonia to give a faint odor. If fertilizer-grade ammonium sulfate is used, the solution may not be clear. In this case, strain through a cloth before using.

This formula has good glow-retardant properties, but is less flame retardant than the first formula. It slightly reduces the strength of treated fabrics.

When ironing treated fabrics, after applying the solution, allow the fabrics to become nearly dry before ironing. Do not redampen with water. Use a moderately hot iron. If the fabric is wet, or the iron is too hot, the solution may stick to the iron. If it does, wipe the iron with a damp cloth.

Fire-Retardant Coatings for Christmas Trees

	Parts by Volume
Sodium silicate (waterglass)	9
Water, containing liquid dishwashing detergent (1 teaspoon per quart)	1

Produces a shiny transparent colorless coating.

or

	Parts by Weight
Sodium silicate (waterglass)	31
China clay	41
Water (containing liquid detergent as above)	28

Produces a cream-colored coating. May be tinted with household dyes.

or

	Parts by Weight
Sodium alginate	1
Monoammonium phosphate	25
China clay	4
Water	70

Produces a frosty white coating. May be tinted with household dyes.

Heat the water to about 180° F., add the sodium alginate, and stir until a uniform gel is obtained. Then add the monoammonium phosphate, heating gently and stirring occasionally until it has dissolved. Finally, add the china clay wet with a little water to a thick paste, and stir until it is uniformly distributed throughout the gel.

Applying the Coatings

Any of the foregoing coatings must be applied heavily. Two coats are more effective than one. Coatings may be applied either by dipping or spraying.

Silver effects can be had by spraying an aluminum paint on trees coated with either the second or the third formula.

Flameproofing Paper and Paperboard

7 pounds borax
3 pounds boric acid
5 pounds diammonium phosphate
13.2 gallons water

Heat the water and dissolve the chemicals in it by stirring continuously as they are added. Cool it to lukewarm temperature before application. The addition of about 1/10 part liquid dishwashing detergent will help penetrate the paper. By immersion, brush, or spray methods, enough should be applied so that the weight of the material when dry will have increased about 15 percent. Test for colorfastness before applying.

or

10 pounds diammonium phosphate
12 gallons water
5 pounds ammonium sulfate

Mix, cool, add detergent, and apply as suggested for the formula above. In humid locations, it may be advisable to include 4 or 5 parts sodium benzoate or sodium propionate.

Fire-Retardant Coatings for Interior Wood

	Percent (by weight)
Basic carbonate white lead	41
Borax	32
Raw linseed oil	22.8
Turpentine	3.6
Japan drier	0.6

Work the white lead into part of the oil, add the rest of the oil and the other ingredients, and stir thoroughly.

Apply 3 or 4 thick coats, or approximately 1 gallon per 125 square feet of surface.

or

	Percent (by weight)
Sodium silicate solution (40-42° Baumé)	31
Kaolin	41
Water	28

Again, 3 or 4 thick coats are necessary, with 4 coats covering about 100 square feet. This paint blisters under fire, producing a nonburning coating.

HUMIDITY INDICATOR

Soak paper toweling or undyed cotton cloth in a strong solution of cobalt chloride in water and let dry; it will turn blue when perfectly dry, then turn pink when it picks up moisture from the air.

SETTING CLOCKS

Formula for remembering how to set clocks for daylight/standard time: Spring forward, fall back.

SWIMMING POOL DISINFECTION

Each time you fill the pool, use 1 quart liquid chlorine bleach (sodium hypochlorite 5 to 6 percent solution) for every 6,000 gallons new water. Allow 7½ gallons water for each cubic foot of pool capacity.

DUSTPROOFING EARTH FOR TRACKS AND TENNIS COURTS

Bare earth can be made dustproof by sprinkling with powdered calcium chloride.

Part VII.
Arts and Crafts

CORNSTARCH "CERAMICS"

1 cup corn starch
1¼ cups cold water
White glue

1 pound bicarbonate of soda
(baking soda)

Blend corn starch and baking soda together thoroughly in a saucepan. Mix in the water and place over medium heat about 4 minutes, stirring constantly, until mixture thickens to mashed potato consistency. Turn out on a plate and cover with a damp cloth until cool.

When easy to handle, knead like dough. Work with one portion at a time, wrapping rest in plastic to prevent drying. Knead a few drops of white glue into pieces of clay for added strength. To make toys, costume jewelry, etc., roll out and cut figures with a knife or shape by hand. When joining pieces, lightly moisten facing parts and press together.

Dry objects on waxed paper for about 36 hours, or until hard.

NONHARDENING MODELING CLAY

67 parts kaolin
33 parts sulfur

60 parts lanolin
40 parts glycerin

Knead together thoroughly. Dry pigments may be worked in for color.

PLAY-DOUGH FOR CHILDREN

1 part flour
1 part salt

Water
Food coloring

Mix the flour and salt; add water to make a thick paste; add coloring. Shapes made of this can be baked and hardened in a slow oven for permanence, although they will be brittle—the major advantage of this formula is that the materials are inexpensive and on hand.

FLOWER CARE

Dyeing Cut Flowers

Use the same packaged dyes used for cloth. Cut the flower stems on a slant. Immerse the stems in water with the dye added.

Keeping Cut Flowers Fresh

Put a pinch of salt in the water.

or

Place an aspirin in the water.

or

Add 2 tablespoons vinegar and 3 tablespoons sugar for each quart of water.

and/or

Snip off the ends of the stems.

DECORATING GLASS

Frosting Glass

Rub the glass with fine sand, powdered glass, or grindstone grit and water in a muslin bag. To decorate with a design, cut out the pattern in paper and glue it on before frosting.

Transferring Prints or Pictures to Glass

Coat the glass with damar varnish or Canada balsam mixed with an equal amount of oil of turpentine; let it dry until it is very sticky—half a day or more. Then soak the printed paper in soft water and lay it on the prepared glass, after first removing surplus water with blotting paper. Press the paper on the glass so that no air bubbles or drops of water remain. Let the paper dry for a full day; then, with wet fingers, rub off the paper. After the paper is removed, another coat of varnish will make the transferred picture more transparent.

PAINT FOR CRAFTWORK OR FINGER PAINTING

For finger painting, block printing, screen painting, stenciling, and brayer printing—or as the binder in pâpier-maché:

½ cup corn starch
1 cup cold water
½ cup mild soap flakes
¼ ounce unflavored gelatin (1 envelope)
2 cups hot water

Combine corn starch and ¾ cup of the cold water in a medium-size saucepan. Soak gelatin in remaining cup of cold water. Add hot water to starch mixture and cook over medium heat, stirring constantly, until mixture comes to a boil and is clear. Remove from heat; blend in gelatin. Add soap and stir until mixture thickens and soap is thoroughly dissolved. To each cup, add and thoroughly stir in 1 teaspoon of household dye. Store in covered jars.

PAPIER-MACHE

Waterproof Trays and Boxes of Papier-Mâché

Paste or glue sheets of paper together in the desired shape and put under heavy pressure; when dry, apply lacquer or japan.

Papier-Mâché Substitute

Make a thick paste of flour and linseed-oil varnish; press it into molds or roll it out, and dry in a hot oven. After the articles are dry, saturate them with linseed oil, then treat with colored lacquer. They will be waterproof.

PLASTER CASTS

Wax Molds for Plaster Casts

4 ounces beeswax
4 ounces corn starch, sifted
1 ounce olive oil

Melt the beeswax over low heat and stir in the olive oil; stir the mixture into the starch until thick as biscuit dough.

The resulting substance will be hard when cold. To use, it must be slightly softened by warming it. Dust the object to be copied with talcum powder; press this object carefully into the wax. The resulting mold may then be filled with the usual plaster-of-paris mixture.

Hardening Plaster-of-Paris Casts

Soak in a solution made by dissolving 1 part alum in 6 parts hot water—at least 1 hour for very small casts, several days for large ones.

To Hasten or Slow the Setting of Plaster of Paris

To hasten, add ½ teaspoon of salt to each pint of water used in mixing the plaster. *To slow,* add 1½ ounces of a saturated solution of borax to each pint of water.

To Clean Plaster Casts

Add enough corn starch to hot water to make a thick paste. Apply a thick layer, still hot; leave overnight to dry. Most of the starch can then be broken off, taking the surface dirt with it. The little remaining starch can be removed with hot water.

Parting Medium for Plaster Mold

4 cubic inches white soap, 1 tablespoon olive oil, 1 pint boiling water. Stir constantly and keep boiling until completely dissolved.

▲ ENGRAVING STEEL

Warm the steel and apply a thin coating of wax evenly over the surface. Use beeswax, hard tallow, or a mixture of equal parts of asphaltum, Burgundy pitch, and beeswax. When the steel has cooled, use a pointed instrument to scratch the design in the wax so that all the wax is removed from the lines that will be engraved. Using an artist's brush, touch the design parts with acid—1 part nitric acid, 1 part hydrochloric acid, and 10

▲**Caution:** *Nitric acid and hydrochloric acid are extremely caustic and should be kept away from skin and clothes.*

parts water. If the effervescence seems too active, add more water. In a few minutes the etching will be done. Dip in hot water to wash off the acid, and clean the surface of the steel by heating it gently and wiping off the wax.

▲CLEANING OLD COINS

For 5 or 10 minutes, immerse silver or bronze coins in a bath of 9 parts distilled water and 1 part sulfuric acid; then plunge them into clear water. Next, wash them with soap, using a soft brush. When they are clean, rinse them once more in clear water, dry with a soft cloth, and rub them gently with a chamois cloth.

▲**Caution:** *Do not spill sulfuric acid on skin or clothes. Can cause severe burns.*

CANDLES

Candle Wick

Carpenter's chalkline is a twisted cotton cord that burns well and makes an excellent wick. To slow its burning rate, soak it overnight in 1 tablespoon salt, 2 tablespoons borax and 1 cup water; then hang it to dry.

Preventing Drips

See page 87 for a formula to prevent candles from dripping.

Color for Homemade Candles

Stir into the melted wax 2 teaspoons of powdered fabric dye for each pound of wax.

Floating Candles

Flat candles molded of whipped wax in gelatin or cookie molds will float in a bowl of water.

SEASHELLS

Cleaning Seashells

Thick encrustations of lime must be picked off with a sharp-edged tool. Dark-colored organic matter on the outer surface of a shell is removed by making a thick mixture of 1 part bleaching powder to 2 parts water, then soaking the shell in the mixture; on removing, wash and scrub it. The shell then must be dipped in an acid bath made of boiling diluted hydrochloric acid—for strong, heavy shells, use 1 part acid to 10 parts water. Dip the shell for a second only, wash and examine; if not enough, give it a second dip. Hold the shell in wooden forceps for dipping. If there is shellac on the shell, it may be removed with alcohol after the acid bath.

▲**Caution:** *Hydrochloric acid is extremely caustic. Do not spill on skin or clothes. Do not breathe the fumes.*

Index

Acids, tests for, 137
Additives
  bread, 25
  canned milk, 50
  cheese, 28
  jelly and jam, 38
Ades, fruit, 36
After-shave lotion, 8
Alkalis, tests for, 137
Alloys, low melting-point, 137
American cheese, 29
Animal horns, care·of, 87
Antiperspirant, 6
Ants, control of, 91, 107
Aphids
  on houseplants, 69
  repellent, mint as, 112
  repellent, nasturtiums as, 112
Apples
  butter, 39
  tree pests, control of, 107
Applesauce, making, 35
Appliances, energy usage of household, 131, 132
Aquarium water, chlorine removal from, 70
Artichoke, Jerusalem, as food, 60
Asparagus, protection for, 107
Automobile
  cleaner, 127
  cooling system cleaner, 128
  polish, 127
  wax, 127

Baby care, 12
Baking
  ingredients, order of, 26
  powder, 35

Banana milk, 48
Barbecue sauce, 42
Barley, whole-wheat egg, 58
Basil
  leaf insecticide, 107
  plant and tomato protection, 107
Bats, control of, 91
Battery
  polarity test, 136
  testing dry-cell, 136
Beans, planting, 108
Bearskin rug, making, 75
Bedbugs, control of, 91
Bee sting pain, relieving, 21
Beetles, control of, 92, 102, 111, 115
Beets, protection for, 108
Bel Paese cheese, 29
Birds, attracting, 125
Biscuit mix, 25, 26
Bites, relieving itch of insect, 21
Bleach, making chlorine, 72
Bloodstain removal, 73
Blue cheese, 29
Books, care of, 86
Bottles, cleaning narrow-necked, 66
Boursin cheese spread, 32
Brass polish, 83
Bread
  additives, 25
  crumbs, Italian, 25
Breakfasts
  instant, 49
  sausages for, 45
  super-strength, 50
Brie cheese, 29
Buckskin
  cleaning, 76
  tanning, 77

152 / INDEX

Burdock as food, 59
Butter
  apple, 39
  peanut, 39

Cabbage, protection for, 108, 109
Cake, 25
  flour, enriched, 35
  ingredients, order of mixing, 26
  mix, 26
Camembert cheese, 29
Candle
  coloring, 149
  drip, preventing, 87
  floating, 149
  wick, 149
Caraway as food, 59
Carpet beetles, control of, 92
Carrot-orange milk, 49
Carrots, protection for, 109
Catnip as pest repellent, 109
Casts. See Plaster casts.
Cat repellents, 127
Cattail as food, 59
Celery, protection for, 110
Cement
  for dental crowns, 9
  for glass, 66
  for marble, 70
Centipedes, control of, 92
Ceramics, cornstarch, 145
Cereals, 27
Cheddar cheese, 29
  spread, 32
Cheese, 28
  chemical additives in, 28
  food, pasteurized process, 28
  spreads, making, 32
  spread, pasteurized process, 28
  storing, 33
Chicken, 46
Chickweed as food, 59
Chicory
  and coffee, 33
  as food, 59
  storing, 110
Chili, 43
Chives, garden uses of, 110

Chlorine
  bleach. See Bleach.
  removal from aquarium water, 70
Christmas trees, fire retardation of, 139
Chrome, polishing, 82
Chocolate milk, 48
Clay, nonhardening modeling, 145
Cleaner
  automobile, 127
  automobile cooling system, 128
  denture, 9
Cleaning
  buckskin, 76
  burned pots, 83
  coins, 149
  furs, 75
  ovens, 84
  plaster casts, 148
  porcelain, 85
  wallpaper, 78
Clothes moths, control of, 92
Clocks, setting time changes in, 141
Cockroaches. See Roaches.
Coffee
  quantities, commercial, 33
  stretchers and substitutes, 33
Coins, cleaning old, 149
Complexion drink, 7
Concord wine, 37
Condensed milk, sweetened, 50
Cookies, 25
  filling for, 27
Cooling with chemicals, 137
Copper polish, 83
Corn, protection of, 110
Cornstarch ceramics, 145
Costs of energy-saving improvements, 135
Cottage cheese, 29, 31
Cotton
  dye, setting, 74
  waterproofing, 74
Cowslip as food, 61
Craftwork paint, 147
Cream, whipped, 50
Cress as food, 60
Crickets, control of, 93
Cucumbers, protection of, 110
Currants, planting, 111

Dandelion
  as food, 60
  wine, 37
Date-nut milk, 48
Dayflower as food, 60
Daylight savings time, formula for, 141
Defogger, windshield and window, 128
Dental
  crowns, cement for, 9
  preparations, 8
Denture
  adhesive, 9
  cleaners, 9
Desserts, gelatin, 39
Diaper stain removal, 72
Dog
  repellents, 127
  urine injury to lawns, 123
Dough, play, 145
Drains, cleaning, 65
Dressings
  harness, 77
  salad, 54, 55
Dill as tomato worm trap, 111
Drinks
  coffee substitute, 33
  fruit, 35
Drug
  interactions, common, 15
  See also Medicine.
Dry-cell battery, testing, 136
Dry cereals, sugar in commercial, 27
Dustproofing earth, 141
Dye
  elderberry leaf, 111
  in cotton, setting, 74
Dyeing
  cut flowers, 145
  furs, 145

Earth, dustproofing, 141
Edam cheese, 30
Eggs, 34
Elderberry leaves, dye from, 111
Electric wire measurements, 134
Electricity
  consumption of household appliances, 131
  magnetic attraction of, 133
Energy
  expenditure table, 10
  saving improvements, 135
Evaporated milk, 50
Evening primrose, 60

Fabric
  care, 72
  fire retardation in, 137
Farmer cheese, 30
Fertilizer burn of lawns, 123
Feta cheese, 30
Files, cleaning metal, 82
Filings, removing metal, 82
Finger painting, 147
Fire
  retardation in fabrics, 137
  retardation of Christmas trees, 139
  retardation of interior wood, 140
  starters, 66
Firearms, 70, 71
Firebrats, control of, 101
Fireplace, fireplaces, 65
  flames, coloring, 65
  flames, increasing, 66
  logs, making free, 65
  stains, removing, 65
Fireweed as food, 60
First aid for common ills, 21
Fish, 40, 47
  and chips, 47
Flameproofing paper and paperboard, 140
Fleas, control of, 93
Flies. *See* Houseflies.
Flours, 34
Floor stain, oak, 80
Flowers
  care of, 145, 146
  dyeing cut, 145
Fluid, lighter, 84
Flypaper, making, 94
Freezer, care of, 85
French dressings, 55
Fruits, 35
  drinks, 35, 36
  stain removal, 72, 73
Fungus diseases, lawn, 117, 118, 119, 120,

121, 122
Furniture, care of, 80, 81
Furs
    cleaning, 75
    dyeing, 75
    softening skins of, 75

Garden care, general, 115
Garlic
    dressing, 55
    as repellent in garden, 108, 111
Gas usage of household appliances, 132
Gelatins, 38, 39
Glass
    care, 66, 67
    cement for, 66
    decorating, 146
Glycerin hand lotion, 7
Gorgonzola cheese, 30
Granola, 28
Grease stain removal, 73
    from books, 86
Great willow herb as food, 60
Green amaranth as food, 61
Gruetzwurst sausage, 44
Gruyère cheese, 30
Guns, care of, 70, 71

Hair
    body builder, 4
    care, 3
    coloring gray, 5
    conditioner for brittle, 3
    conditioner for dry, 3
    highlights for, 4
    rinse for peroxided, 4
    treatment for damaged, 4
    wave set, 4
Hamburgers, cooking, 42
Hand care, 5
Harness dressing, 77
Herbs, 38
Hiccups, curing, 21
Horns, care of animal, 87
House flies, control of, 94
Household appliances, energy usage of, 131, 132
Houseplants
    care of, 67
    pests on, 68
    soil aeration for, 67
    soil sterilization for, 67
    watering, 67, 68
Humidity indicator, 141

Ills, first aid for common, 21
Ingredients, remembering order of baking, 26
Ink
    stain removal, 73
    for stone or marble, 70
Insect
    bites, relieving itch of, 21
    pests, lawn, 123
    repellents, 98, 99, 115
    traps, 116
Insecticide, basil leaf, 107
Insomnia, herbal baths for, 10
Iron stain removal, 73
Italian
    bread crumbs, 25
    sausage, 45
Itch, relieving insect bite, 21

Japanese beetles
    control of, 111
    zinnias as traps for, 115
Javelle water, 72
Jellies and jams, 38
Jerusalem artichoke as food, 60
Jewelweed for poison ivy rash, 112

Kale pests, control of, 112
Kindling, fragrant, 66

Lamb's quarters as food, 60
Lawns
    buried debris and, 124
    burns, 123
    care, 117
    causes of poor, 120
    damage and compacted soils, 124
    diseases, fungus, 117, 118, 119, 120
    dog urine injury to, 123
    fertilizer burn of, 123
    fungi, control of, 121, 122

grasses, undesirable mixtures of, 123
insect pests, 123
mowing of, 124
pesticide injury to, 123
pythium diseases, 118
runners on, 124
slime molds, 120
snow molds, 119
watering of, 124
Leather care, 76
Lecithin, use of, 40
Lighter fluid, 84
Limburger cheese, 30
Lotion
after-shave, 8
hand, 5, 6
skin lanolin, 7
sunburn, 22

Maggots, radishes and control of, 114
Mallow as food, 60
Marble
care of, 69, 70
cement for, 70
ink for, 70
stain removal, 69
Marigolds
marsh, as food, 61
as nematode repellents, 113
as pest deterrents, 112
Mascara, 6
Mayonnaise, 53, 54, 55
Mealybugs on houseplants, 68
Meat, 40
browning aids, 43
products, contents of, 40
sauces, 42
storage, 41
tenderizer, 40
Medicines,
learning about, 13
storage of, 15
Metal
care, 82
files, cleaning, 82
filings, removing, 82
Mice, control of, 95, 112, 117
Mildew stain removal, 73

Milk
additives in canned, 50
chocolate, 48
banana, 48
carrot-orange, 48
date-nut, 48
evaporated, 50
flavored, 48
hot wheat, 48
and milk products, 48
molasses, 48
peanut, 48
shake, Seattle delight, 49
substitute, 50
tomato, 48
vanilla, 48
Milkweed, 61
as pest trap, 112
Mint as aphid repellent, 112
Mirrors, washing, 67
Mites, control of, 69, 95
Modeling clay, nonhardening, 145
Molasses milk, 48
Mole repellents, 112, 117
Monterrey Jack cheese, 30
Mosquitos, control of, 96, 97, 98
Moths
control of clothes, 92
repellent, sweet woodruff as, 115
Mozzarrella cheese, 30
Muenster cheese, 30
Mushrooms, lawn, 120
Mustard, homemade, 38

Nail care, 5, 6
Nasturtiums as aphid repellents, 112
Nectars, fruit, 36
Nematode repellents, 113
Nerve preparations, 9, 10
Nettle spray, garden, 115
Nickel tarnish, preventing, 82
Nitroglycerin tablets, storage of, 15
Noodles, whole-wheat eggless, 58

Oak
darkening, 79
floor stain, 80
Odor removal from pots, 84

Oil and vinegar dressing, 54
Onions as pest repellents, 113
Oven
    temporary brick, 84
    care of, 84

Pain. *See* Ills, Itches.
Paint handcraft, 147
Pancakes
    freezing, 52
    mixes, 52
    syrups and toppings, 53
Pantry pests, control of, 99
Paper, flameproofing, 140
Paperboard, flameproofing, 140
Papier-mâché, 147
    substitute, 147
Parsley as protective plant, 113
Parsnips, storage of, 113
Pasta, 56, 58
Paste, wallpaper, 78
Play dough, 145
Peanut
    butter, 39
    milk, 48
Peaches, preventing discoloration of cut, 36
Peas, planting, 113
Perspiration stain removal, 73
Pesticide
    injury to lawns, 123
    for wood beetles, 103
Pest repellent
    catnip as, 109
    marigolds as, 112
    rosemary as, 114
    tansy as, 114
    thyme as, 114
    turnips as, 115
Pests
    control of pantry, 99
    lawns insect, 123
Pets, care of, 70
Piano keys, whitening, 85
Pigweed as food, 61
Plants and birds, preferred, 125
Plaster casts
    cleaning, 148
    hardening, 148
    wax molds for, 147
Plaster mold, parting medium for, 148
Poison ivy
    jewelweed for rash of, 112
    relieving itch of, 21
Polish
    automobile, 127
    brass, 83
    copper, 83
    and wax, comparison of wood, 80
    wood, 81
Porcelain cleaning, 85
Port-Salut cheese, 31
Potatoes, protection for, 113
Pot cheese, 31
Pots
    cleaning burned, 83
    odor removal from, 84
Poultry, 40
Prescription Latin, reading, 13
Protein foods, 42
Provolone cheese, 31
Purslane as food, 61

Rabbit repellent, 114, 117
Radishes and maggot control, 114
Rats, control of, 99
Red spider on houseplants, 69
Refrigerator deodorizing, 85
Relish, green tomato, 58
Rhubarb, growing, 114
Rice, 56, 58
    brown, 59
Ricotta cheese, 31
Roaches, control of, 100
Romano cheese, 31
Roquefort cheese, 31
    dip, 33
    dressing, 55
Rose hip juice, 36
Rosemary as pest repellent, 114
Rust
    removal, 83
    stain removal, 73

Saddle soap, 76
Salad
    dressings, 53

sprouts, growing, 57
Sauces, meat, 42
Sausages, 43, 44
Scale on houseplants, 69
Scalp, conditioner for dry, 4
Scorpions, control of, 100
Seashells, cleaning, 149
Seasonings, 38
Seattle delight milkshake, 49
Shampoo, 3
Shaving cream, brushless, 7
Sherbert, yogurt, 52
Short circuit, locating a, 133
Shortening, vegetable, 56
Silver
    polishing, 84
    storage of, 84
Silverfish, control of, 101
Skin care, 7
Soap, 78
    hand, 5
    rinsing out, 78
    saddle, 76
Soil
    aerating houseplant, 67
    and lawn damage, compacted, 124
    quality, changing, 117
    sterilizing houseplant, 67
Sorrel as food, 61
Soufflés, vegetable, 56
Spaghetti sauce, 43
Spiders, control of, 101
Sprouts for salad, growing, 57
Squashes, protection for, 114
Stain
    for gun barrels, bluing, 71
    oak floor, 80
Stain removal, 72
    blood, 73
    from books, 86
    from fireplaces, 65
    grease, 73
    ink, 73
    from marble, 69
    mildew, 73
    perspiration, 73
    rust, 73
    from tan shoes, 76
    wine, 72, 73
    from wood, 81
Standard time formula, 141
Steel, engraving, 148
Stone, ink for, 70
Storage
    cheese, 33
    chicory, 110
    meat, 41
    medicines, 15
    parsnips, 113
    silver, 84
Sunburn lotion, 22
Swedish sausage, 44
Sweet woodruff as moth repellent, 115
Swimming pool disinfection, 141
Swiss cheese, 31
Syrups, pancake, 53

Tansy as pest repellent, 114
Teeth. *See* Dental, Tooth.
Temperature scales, conversion factors for, 136
Tennis courts, dustproofing earth for, 141
Termites, control of, 102
Thistle as food, 61
Thyme as pest repellent, 114
Ticks, control of, 102
Tomato, tomatos
    basil plant protection for, 107
    milk, 48
    relish, green, 58
    protection for, 114
    worms, dill as trap for, 111
Tooth powder, 8
Traps, insect, 116
Turnips
    as pest repellents, 115
    protection for, 115

Vanilla milk, 48
Vegetables, 56
    shortening, 56
    soufflés, 56
Veneer, repair of wood, 81

Wallpaper
    cleaning, 78

paste, 78
Wart removers, 22
Wasps, control of, 102
Water, chlorine removal from aquarium, 70
Watering lawns, 124
Waterproofing fabrics, 74
Wax
    automobile, 127
    and polish, comparison of wood, 80
    stain removal from books, 86
    wood, 80
Weeds, edible, 59
Weevil repellent, 115
Wheat milk, hot, 48
Whipped cream, 50
Whitewash, 79
Whole-wheat
    biscuit mix, 26
    egg barley, 58
    eggless noodles, 58
    flour, 35
Wild portulaca as food, 61

Windows, washing, 67
Wine
    making, 37
    stain removal, 72, 73
Wiring
    locating short circuit in, 133
    measurements, 134
Wood
    care, 79
    fire retardation of interior, 140
    polishes and waxes, 80
    repairs on, 81, 82
    stain removal from, 81
Woodchuck repellent, 115
Wool, testing for, 74
Woolen fabric, waterproofing, 74

Yarrow as pest repellent, 115
Yogurt
    making, 51
    popsicles, 51
    sherbert, 52

Zinnias as Japanese beetle traps, 115